Justice, Grief, and Christ's Pathways to Wholeness

Justice, Grief, and Christ's Pathways to Wholeness

Edited by
JAMES GODDARD

with an afterword by John W. de Gruchy

WIPF & STOCK · Eugene, Oregon

JUSTICE, GRIEF, AND CHRIST'S PATHWAYS TO WHOLENESS

Wipf & Stock
An Imprint of Wipf and Stock Publishers
199 W. 8th Ave., Suite 3
Eugene, OR 97401

www.wipfandstock.com

PAPERBACK ISBN: 979-8-3852-5717-1
HARDCOVER ISBN: 979-8-3852-5718-8
EBOOK ISBN: 979-8-3852-5719-5

02/05/26

Contents

Introduction

James Goddard

A BOOK OF JOURNEYS

The idea for this book formed in October 2023 on a perfect spring evening at dusk, in the cooling dust of Nieu Bethesda in the Karoo. We had just heard a piano recital in an art gallery open to the street and an evening breeze. In pauses between cadences of freshly composed music, the last dusk chorus of doves and starlings accompanied the soloist, like nature's perfectly syncopated orchestra, while an Irish wolfhound wandered in, as characterful as a village afficionado from the street. After walking with me a block to their home to taste Cape wine at their fireplace, and as we sat down to supper in their *voorkamer*, the *gasvry* hospitality of Charl and Belinda du Toit is where this book began.

As we enjoyed a traditional Karoo supper, Charl and Belinda spoke words of compassion to this grieving traveler on his way home, still wrestling with what lay ahead. My wife and I were in conversations to end our marriage. Charl reflected transparently on his grief in losing his first marriage, and he meandered, as he can, into a most convincing exegesis of David and Solomon and Abishag the Shunammite in Song of Solomon! Being the dominee at heart that he is, he then came to his spontaneous sermon's application: "Isn't that what it's all about? We don't get our love right and we don't get it requited all the way through life—because only in Christ can love be perfected, and only in Christ will love be requited."[1] Charl's timeless truth turned out to be both the seed and then the kernel of this book.

An epiphany that had dawned partially along my journey to the Western Cape was now fully revealed, in loving words and a memorable meal. I had courage to return home, to an ending marriage, with new hope—that even though we love imperfectly and incompletely in life, there is yet opportunity to find Christ truly present in our human predicaments, to help us complete something kind and faithful and beautiful, something *whole*, in the learning curve we undergo into knowing God and God's all-redeeming love.

At dawn the next morning, just before reaching the turning to Cradock, an idea of mini autobiographies and the title of this book came to me, almost simultaneously with the names of the men I would phone to write it. Thus, a historian-theologian finding his way into the Anabaptist tradition, telephoned Faure Louw, Laurie Gaum, and Cobus van Wyngaard, three pastor-theologians, and Rex van Vuuren, a psychologist-philosopher, all of whom found their way into faith from their Dutch Reformed backgrounds.[2] Would they write? To my surprise, they were each willing to craft a chapter on my suggested theme of justice, grief, and Christ's pathways to wholeness.

As I know them, each writer has confronted the social injustice of apartheid in different eras and has found ways to break with that crime against humanity that so traumatized South African society. Each has been formed in a deepening faith, through trauma and grief, along pathways towards hope, integration, and wholeness. My invitation was for each to narrate a significant part of his journey of faith into this wholeness, to remember experiences,

1. This conversation I recorded later that evening, in my journal.

2. Faure Louw and Rex van Vuuren I met during my years in the Students' Christian Association at the University of the Witwatersrand (Wits) in the early 1980s. They each appear in different capacities in my PhD research findings about the history of SCA. See Goddard, "Invitations to Prophetic Integrity." Laurie Gaum and Cobus van Wyngaard are more recent colleagues, since 2011.

and to record stories in creative autobiographical, theological, or philosophical reflection.

So began a delightful year of meeting on WhatsApp, reading, discussing, agreeing, and then gathering face-to-face in May 2024, for a working week in Elarduspark, Pretoria, as we labored to create this volume. We were agreed on a common assumption—followers of Christ and all people of faith need new boldness to respond *in their faith* to injustices in the world that have led to the current meta crisis of hastening authoritarianism and creeping fascism, state capture, regional wars, widening inequality, the global cost-of-living-crisis, and climate collapse. The challenge of this moment is to disrupt and transform injustices that oppress and traumatize the weakest people in our world—injustices that have deep roots in our history. This challenge represents an unprecedented prophetic invitation for Christians and people of faith, worldwide.

In response to this challenge, our guiding question became: *How have white, generationally privileged Christians in South Africa responded in our context to Christ's invitation to act justly, love mercifully, and live humbly into authentic wholeness, embodying the faith of Christ among the marginalized, rather than subscribing to faith in Christ from a position of power?*

Our shared South African context is one of longed-for reparation—to restore what has been stolen and repair what has been broken by the injustices of apartheid.[3] This ongoing hope points towards a not-yet-realized reconciliation. In our need for healing in South Africa's wounded history, there is a role for winsome, transparent narrations of stories, of successes and failures, by followers of Jesus and people of faith who are finding our way into living more justly. Imaginations need to be sparked by stories of

3. The painful reopening of the Cradock Four Inquest as we finalized this manuscript, and the public statement of white South African Christians responding to Afrikaner "refugees" so publicly welcomed into the United States, are merely two examples of generational injustices still crying out for prophetic voices and actions to enable reparation and healing of the apartheid ills that continue to compound in our wounded present. For more on the inquest, see Clarke, "Cradock Four Inquest." For the statement by South African white Christian leaders, see Southern Cross, "White SA Church Leaders."

ordinary courage and weakness in the face of injustice, trauma, and grief. Hearts need to find hope in the mystery of Christ's pathways to healing, authenticity, wholeness, and peace.

We offer a book, then, that integrates autobiography, theology, philosophy, and spirituality, to Christ followers and people of faith who need inspiration in this moment of chronic social and political disintegration, to bring "a life lived"[4] into closer correlation with Jesus' lived life—Jesus' politics of justice, grief, and wholeness. Each author's chapter describes his evolving faith journey, reflects on his responses to social injustice, narrates something of his pathways through trauma and grief, and reflects on his invitation by Christ or the Divine, to become authentically whole.

Early in the process, there were to-be-expected debates: *How, James, can we write about wholeness wholly, if no women have been invited to join our conversations as coauthors? Why only white men and no black writers, to throw into relief our stories of white privilege?* There were no formulaic answers to these vital questions from any of us. For me, it was simple. The idea for the book and the men who should write it came to me unbidden, and I was prompted to act.

Each of the chapters to follow is therefore an autobiographical vignette, composed in response to the title. The result is a rich exploration of memory, experience, perspective, and insight from four white South African men of very different walks of life, who do life at very different ages, from forty years of age to eighty. Forty is the biblical number signifying *completion*, so there is something holistic about this range of ages and experience.

In our conversation about why and how and what to write, our political debates around gender and race have been our longest, and our conversations continue unresolved. For me as editor, our most significant conversation has been about *who Jesus is* in the Scriptures and *how Jesus meets us* with divine grace in our shared commitment to faith—in the history and continuing injustice

4. Cobus van Wyngaard's phrase, as in his chapter below, from his younger perspective.

of structural inequality in South Africa; in our sorest griefs and losses; in the day-to-day pathways to wholeness of our spirituality; and in our future hopes. In response to my gently posed *Jesus question*, moments of awkwardness were felt as we negotiated an obstinate truth—we are diversely formed in convictions, from slightly different traditions of faith, whether Anabaptist, Protestant Reformed, or interfaith.

The hospitable space that we created after this acknowledgement has enabled conversations to continue, unresolved, about how best to take hold of this Jesus, his place in the stories of our lives, and in the title of this book. Within such a healthy, creative tension, our conversations have touched on whether Jesus is one of, or a combination of the following: ethical guide, archetypal stranger, source of life-transforming compassion, or the One who, living still, wants to be known and to know us "from the side."[5]

The creative diversity of our experiences and different points of view about Jesus of Nazareth makes the outpouring of autobiography in this volume a richer, more compelling record of four uniquely different faith journeys. Each of the authors has been shaped either by looking to Jesus, or by looking around or even beyond Christ as their source or goal or inspiration, on their singularly different and yet commonly human pathways through grief, disorientation, and tears, towards integration, hope, healing, wholeness, and peace.

A theme common to all the chapters is the role of the church in the lives of the writers—in their formation; in social injustices that caused woundedness; or in helping them along their pathways towards wholeness. In this way, our book celebrates, questions, and even reappraises the church's vocation to be a community that models and mediates Jesus' politics of justice, healing, and wholeness to society.

Associated with the church theme are two related themes: salvation-conversion, and the nature of our human soul. The authors describe salvation and conversion as far from instantaneous, but rather as a sequence of moments of radical transformation in

5. Another insight from Cobus van Wyngaard, in what follows.

relation to Jesus, justice, and wholeness in society. As the autobiographies unfold, there is also a varied yet composite exploration of the geographies of the soul—that inner territory that extends out of embodiment, emotions, memories, personalities, histories, places, and sacred stories and reaches beyond imaginings shaped by faith, myths, and dreams towards the near and far horizons of hope.

The richest theme that recurs through this autobiographical collection is that of the disruption of trauma, and the new life that such disruption can bring in its wake. These pages revisit different traumatic disruptions, among them a deportation; a defrocking; and deaths of dear ones loved—all of which have caused the most profound experiences of grief, loss, and human disorientation. But in this book, there are also many instances of fruitful disruption, like a sudden, new perspective that debunked apartheid's deceptive and fraudulent ideology—the dropping of apartheid scales from eyes that can now only see *through* race, as an icon that points into God's deeper reality.

In my view, all the holy disruptions described in these pages are just that—holy—because they are embraced as integral to faith in Jesus Christ or to faith in God per se, by each pilgrim in this company. The grit recorded here, of honestly facing and working through life's disruptions, is not unlike the very human struggle of Jesus himself and of the first disciples, who learned to walk faithfully through traumas and griefs no matter the cost, into the wholeness and fullness of life promised by God, whom they called Shepherd of Israel.

Another emerging theme throughout these chapters is the earthy connection of each writer to a particular place in South Africa—if you like, each author's deep sense of being *in place* in our country and its unfolding story. Whether the writers were placed in remote, semirural Limpopo; in affluent Elarduspark in Pretoria; in cosmopolitan, inner city congregations of Cape Town or Pretoria; in a childhood home in Swaziland; or in the physical and spiritual landscapes of academia, the vocation of each writer has been realized while experiencing injustices that violated *their belonging* to particular South African places—a rural town, an inner-city community or congregation; or even the geographical, cultural, devotional, biophysical, or professional places that enable our flourishing as human beings.

One more thread interwoven through this collection is its spirituality—the writers' free outpourings of heartfelt, bold, probing, and provocative questions, prayers, or laments. There are elephant-in-the room type questions, while others appear obvious at first. Their questions are almost never rhetorical but are recorded passionately, to carry forward the plots of four narratives in four stories. And then there are spontaneous prayers and imaginary letters from the heart. As editor, I chose to italicize all the writers' many questions, prayers, laments, or vicarious letters recorded throughout the book, because the spirituality expressed in them illustrates the agency, passion, teachability, bafflement, and hope that arise whenever and however Jesus or the Divine encounters us in our humanity. More significantly, every expression of spirituality recorded here, in questions, prayers, or imaginative utterances, is penned always in tandem with the *politics* of true faith: *How then shall we build, relate, love, and live, to embody the wholeness, justice, and peace of Jesus in a fractious world?*

There were many options in which to sequence the chapters. With my training as a historian, I chose to present them in chronological order by age, so that the younger writers get to speak before their elders. The natural increment of reach, range of memory, and maturity of perspective, in this chronological sequence, are a rewarding feature of this book, where the two eldest writers are old enough to be the fathers or even the grandfathers of the two youngest.

This has been my first experience of editing a prose book that is somewhat scholarly. I am indebted to each of my fellow authors for their kindness as I tried to honor the heartbeat of their literary intentions. In the labors of this project, the scope and magnitude of an editor's calling and responsibility are now more than plain to me. Therefore, I take ownership, after all my best efforts, for any editorial shortfalls that remain.

The synergy and robust agreement in essentials throughout our shared creative process are a joy to have experienced. I extend heartfelt thanks to my fellow pilgrims who have written so generously; to Charl and Belinda du Toit for your shepherding role in the genesis of this book; to Huma Louw for hosting us graciously in your home in Pretoria; and to the financial donors in South Africa and Canada who made possible our joint meeting and the writing and publishing of this volume. Matt Wimer at Wipf and Stock has our shared gratitude for every kind assistance as a wonderfully human publisher. This volume was peer-reviewed by two specialists in the field of theology. Thank you to Kobus Schoeman for stepping in sacrificially, at the last minute, to facilitate a blind peer review of the chapters! Great thanks, Klippies Kritzinger, for welcoming our manuscript and writing a commendation. And before last, particular thanks to John de Gruchy for pondering these stories in your apt and insightful Afterword. Your gift of precious time and wise words speak of that almost bygone gracious age in the Academy, when neither every minute nor every page of writing was monetized. Lastly, we thank all who take up this book and read, on pilgrim pathways in the steps of our savior Jesus Christ, through injustice and grief, to wholeness and peace.

Lent 2025

CHAPTER ONE

Midlife Pauses and Everyday Justice

Cobus van Wyngaard

DRAWN TO EVERYDAY LIFE

There is a centuries-old genre of spiritual writing that focuses on the spiritual heroes. The martyrs. Those who performed near-impossible feats of Christian witness, who changed the course of history. Walk through the local Christian bookstore and you'll find that this genre continues to sell.

The words below are not that.

My high school life revolved around the church and church-related activities. Whether it was youth groups at school or at church, weekly meetings, or holiday camps. Sometimes participating and sometimes leading, mentoring, and being mentored. Those weeks and years of community and reflection inevitably made me who I became. Much of what happened then, and in the broader formation that these events were embedded into, I had to unlearn. I continue that work of unlearning. But I also learned much. To pretend that the person I am could have existed without those experiences would be a lie. They are at the heart of much of the words that follow.

I remember one conversation, the kind that those who have been part of such spaces will know well, where the adult volunteer who facilitated our discussion worked to reorient our lives towards greater Christian purpose. It was an evening youth group in a sterile high school classroom, attended by a small group for whom this Christian community filled a weeknight of our teenage programs. The exact words have long faded from memory, but the basic question was what we wanted to do with our lives. Looking back, I can now see it as the inevitable question that probably directs much of modern adolescence. Everything was formed to orient us towards a future as adults—and faith had to be intertwined with this quest. My answer was an abstract but optimistic claim that I wanted to "change the world." The volunteer asked me why. I cannot recall the conversation exactly, but her question stayed with me. *Why would I want to change anything?* It would take me many years of study to discover just how much destruction was wrought by people of faith who wanted to change the world.

I don't think her question was meant to send me down that uncomfortable path. She certainly was not thinking about the history of church-sanctioned colonialism, where the church-sanctioned call to form the world in the image of Europe resulted in death and destruction on an unprecedented scale. She could not have imagined the contemporary insights around how modern wars are always justified by the belief that we are making the world better—and that some people unfortunately need to be sacrificed as part of this quest. So runs the repeated logic of the powerful.[1] At most, her intention was to instill some Christian humility to counter my teenage hubris. Whatever her intention, she did provide a brief counterweight to much of popular Christianity.

It's not that I don't want the world to be changed. It's not that I refuse to put my weight behind changing it—or at least small parts of it. It's just that the meditations written here grew in a different direction.

The more I grappled with the questions prompting the words that follow—about grief, justice, and wholeness—the more I was drawn into realities that drive my everyday life: getting kids to school, being a decent parent, clearing away an inbox and calendar,

1. Gray, *Black Mass*, 107–45.

teaching students, balancing budgets—in brief, doing life. If anything, I try to be honest about the mundane in my everyday life, about the very particular place that following Jesus draws me into, and about being white and upper-middle class and increasingly conscious of what this means.

I feel the need to be honest both about Jesus and about this upper-middle-class existence, so I start by trying to sketch out the times, places, and formative experiences out of which I am writing. This is not a full-length biography, because that's not the point of this volume. At most, my paragraphs are glimpses into contexts that locate where I reflect from, my attempt at shedding light on where my words emerge from—a life story in a very specific geographic location, and at a particular stage of life. Reflecting on grief, justice (and Jesus), and wholeness, to some extent, weaves together parts of my theological work from the past years and parts of my life lived for some past decades.

ON THE PARTICULARITY OF WRITING (ABOUT GOD)

I look on a small pile of my past writings scattered across my bookshelf and computer folders. Mostly dry words in academic articles. Others, more passionate calls, written for smaller audiences of friends. A collection of sermons where I have written out the full text of what I intended to say. *What do I do when I do theology? What am I doing when writing here?* Increasingly, I think of my words as an attempt at taking the location from which we write seriously. Specifically, to take *place* seriously when we attempt to write about that "which we call God."[2] The hesitancy with which the Belgic Confession speaks about the naming of God, recognizing the constraints in the human act of naming, has characterized my own theological work through many years—the honest recognition that it is *humans* who do the naming. Our audacity of naming, when we know that our human words can

2. Christian Reformed Church, *Belgic Confession*, article 1.

never fully conceptualize that "which we call God." But what the Belgic Confession could not yet clearly see, is that humans speak about God from vastly different places, and we are thus left with a rich tapestry of different views on the God we name. My words over the years have been a small part of an attempt at making sense of the particularity of my places, and my placement. These words here try to clarify this particularity-in-place of my own writing.

One of the most unique phrases from the Confession of Belhar comes from article 4, where justice is being reflected on, and the church is called to "stand where God stands."[3] There are limited biblical or confessional precedents for this call. The idea is not novel, but Belhar's specific formulation is rather unique. These words have found a place on pulpit cloths and in the church buildings of the Dutch Reformed Church and the Uniting Reformed Church in the inner city of Pretoria. We place them on our pulpits as a reminder of our own commitment to the slow work of undoing the legacy of apartheid.

Our positioning—where we stand—implies a spatial imagination. God is somewhere. God stands in a place. With people located there. Yes, God is also in all places, but the God of whom I try to write is a God who stands *in particular places*. And it is from a particular place that I try to write about this God.

How do I remain conscious of the "place in which I am," when thinking about the God I am called to stand alongside? Mostly, place can be described geographically—located on a map but viewed from where we are slowly passing: the plants, the buildings, the open spaces between, and, always, the people, who give meaning to these places. *Always the people.* Over the past decades we have most often viewed these constituent parts through the windows of our moving technologies, which connect us so readily to places—the bird's-eye view from an airplane window, the view from a train, bus, or car. Sometimes we are not even viewing from the windows of fast-moving modes of transport but through our electronic screens and apps, looking at street views and short video reels. Increasingly distant. Seldom viewed at the speed of walking. Seldom

3. Dutch Reformed Church, "Confession of Belhar," article 4.

viewed from the limited perspective that our human bodies effect when we allow our senses alone to fully take in the places in which we find ourselves.

As much as cosmology reminds us of just how insignificant our place in the universe might be, as much as geology reminds us of just how brief our time on this earth has been, and as much as ecotheology reminds us of the devastation brought about by the human and ethical risks of centering the human, for me it is always *the people* who draw my attention. In my theological work, I have found myself increasingly drawn over time to the social. While others would look at how our faith intersects with what happens inside of us—in our bodies and psyches—for me the questions of faith have always moved me towards what happens between us. *What happens in community and communities? What happens in relationships and conflicts? What happens between people when we are groups?*

But we've never been able to just be people living with people. We group people. And in a modern world, with technologies that connect places, carrying people across space at tremendous speeds, our identities seldom refer to any permanent connection with particular places. Perhaps this connection does happen in some abstract way, as when nation states hand out passports, based on legal status, in a particular geographically defined area. But connection with place seldom happens in the concrete sense, where plants, buildings, and the open spaces in between remind us of who *the people* moving between them really are.

So, we tend to identify people through the visible markers they carry on their bodies and how we read those into the history of peoplehood, or by the ideas that they stand for and how those relate to power and the powerful in a specific time. It is not accidental that the markers I carry, which in South Africa identify me as "white," are those that, under another political climate, were differently named as "European." I was allowed (or was made) to be named, as from a different part of the globe—or rather, my body carried this other part of the globe across space into the southern part of Africa. I was allowed (or was made) to be from another place, while living life in this place, because of what my body represented.

That representation—being white—at least as part of a visible identity,[4] and as far more than a mere visual marker, is always present in my reflections. It must be, given that across the pages of this book, we writers are gathered largely around a particular white, Afrikaans, Reformed identity. This, too, is always present—being ordained in the Dutch Reformed Church. I am a dominee.

But two less obvious parts of who I am will perhaps become even more visible in the pages that follow. First, I am located in the inner city of Pretoria. Sunnyside. A name that, for those familiar with Pretoria, may evoke some visceral responses—regarding crime, poverty, white flight, urban decay. A place to be avoided. A place pulsating with life. As with many places that people call home, my being drawn into Sunnyside started out as a combination of convenience, affordability, and social identification. It became home only in time. It continues to become a place from which I am becoming.

Second, these words are slowly taking form on both sides of my fortieth birthday. My birthdays have seldom had much symbolic meaning over the past decades—one more day that comes and goes. Our children go to school; a semester needs to start. But this year's transition was different. I'm aware of years that have passed by. I'm even more aware of the years that are still to come. In some ways, my reflections here are deeply intertwined with this transition.

I write from a different stage of life than that of my coauthors. This reality has been deeply impressed on me throughout many hours of conversation that have formed this book. I don't write these words because my particular location detracts from the writing process, but exactly because my particular place informs the words—in a cityscape on the Highveld, between particular buildings and trees, where I am an ill-fitting but inevitable member of multiple groups, carrying identities chosen or bestowed: a person situated in time and at a particular stage of life. Somehow, I need

4. Alcoff, *Visible Identities*.

to reveal these fragments[5] of my life to you if I hope that you will understand my thoughts. Call it midlife. *Crisis?*

GRIEVING FOR THE WORLD

I cannot imagine living in a different time—the time and the world that most of my coauthors are writing from. Nothing in me wishes to have lived in that earlier time. I've never been a nostalgic person. And our particular past is not something I would wish to return to. *Die goeie ou dae* (the good old days) hold little that is good or golden for me. I came of age as the dot-com bubble was bursting, and the internet was exploding. I entered university when computer labs providing internet were only just being rolled out. I graduated with Facebook and Twitter on a phone just as this Web 2.0 idyll of decentralized authorship, with its endless stream of theological reflections on blogs, was starting to lose its shine.

I come from an age and class where grief seems to have been postponed for most of us. Infant mortality in South Africa is a fraction of what it was just a few generations ago. What killed my grandparents will likely be resolved with a small medical procedure in my own lifetime. Even with horrific wars raging as I type—Palestine, Ukraine, Congo, Sudan—these feel far away, and their impacts are felt in petrol prices rather than in the real fear that *my* children will be drafted to fight or be put in mortal danger. The privileged classes of my generation seem to have found ways of passing through the first few decades of life in ways that limited personal trauma, to an extent unimaginable for past generations. Those same privileged classes continue to promise that bodily integrity regarding food security, healthcare, and an end to violence is in the very next wave of our development cycle, or within reach, in just a few more decades.

But when I scrutinize this contemporary tendency of grief delayed, there is something hidden that must be revealed. Underneath our veneer of self-sufficiency, there is an explosion in

5. Jennings, *After Whiteness*, 23–46.

antidepressants and the silence and shame related to intimate violence that invades homes. Even where the markings of a middle-class existence are in place through education and connections, a morbid dread of unemployment, or the imminent threat in potential unemployment, and how that brutal economic calculus can shatter stability in an instant, seem to impact all of life. Everything in life can end up being directed at just warding off this threatening possibility.

From the global north, the Offspring shouted our frustration through their hit "The Kids Aren't Alright," with an apparent lack of purpose that ensued from their idealistic world. From the first verse, they proclaim the grief of losing the possibilities they imagined for themselves when they were young. Although released in my eighth-grade year, it took some decades for these words to ring true for me. The bright future that was promised growing up, both individually and in the promised miracle called the democratic South Africa, seldom delivered. In many ways, these hopeful aspirations just became stale.

But it is more than staleness that my midlife perspective detects. I pass through this stage of life knowing that the future will likely bring the need for grief, in ways that the first decades of my life could not prepare me for. With each passing year, the possibility of a parent outliving a child increases. The chances that a life partnership imagined as lasting for decades may end early are reduced to technical calculations by actuaries in insurance companies, and are presented only as numbers on a life cover quotation. But perhaps most importantly, the world staggers on the brink of collapse under the consequences of inherent contradictions created by the super-wealthy, who cannot dare to share their wealth. And the earth simmers under increasing temperatures, the implications of which we can postpone just far enough into the future to proceed with life as normal, for another orbit around the sun.

How do we live in this in-between space—between a life where grief can be postponed, and the ongoing fear that this fragile compromise might come crashing down onto us, bringing with it the death and destruction that we were not prepared to face throughout our lives? Is that perhaps part of what gave rise to a surge in the postapocalyptic and dystopian literature on which we became adults? Was the explosion into our lives of stories such as The Hunger Games, Parable of the Sower, *or* Station Eleven *perhaps an attempt to find resources for what we fear we may need to live through?*

Yet still, I cannot imagine living in that different time that most of my coauthors lived through and are reflecting on. I am a child of the transition to democracy. I was formed by the thirty years of democracy in South Africa. My entire life has been directed at making sense of exactly this. And although the world celebrated this transition, I write in the past tense because the celebration seems to have faded of late, and I grapple with a surprising anger. There is a loss that I must put into words.

I express my loss hesitantly. It cannot compare to the disillusionment of millions for whom freedom remains out of reach. My anger probably has little place in the greater scheme of things. But allow it its place. *Why was I brought into a world at a time and place where I was made to be a stranger to those who could have been friends, even family?* I cannot see this world without a deep sense of sadness about uninitiated relationships over the years, or limited relationships into the present. Apartheid and its afterlife have determined where I should be and whom I should be with.

I must acknowledge how I benefited personally from apartheid—as the grandson of a boilermaker and the son of a PhD holder, I am the product of apartheid social mobility for whites in South Africa. *But how do I then name the loss? How do I grieve the relationships that could have been but never were? How do I allow for the anger, because the church that should have been the place to teach me this grief has never really grieved about what was broken, or even truly named it as broken?* Maybe this was because the church was also the cause of that illness for which it should have provided a cure.

Could it have been different? I grew up in Swaziland, in the rural community of Nhlangano. White families could be counted on one set of fingers and toes. For us, as white people in a numerical minority, moving around Nhlangano seldom evoked any of the white South African anxieties associated with such a position. This memory suggests that there may have been a different status quo in Nhlangano. However, even in this community, distinctly different from apartheid in many ways, white people lived in a world apart. Even without apartheid laws, "Whites Only" signs, or "White Areas," racial hierarchies and boundaries were maintained, nonetheless. Apartheid, after all, was but a blip on the much longer trajectory of colonialism, which reinterpreted every inch of the world through a pseudo-racial calculus.

It would require decades of unlearning and counter formation for me to perceive, in retrospect, how truly disrupted the community life of Nhlangano was. Underneath the idyllic picture of small-town freedom of movement, a brutal logic was maintained. It was not in the spatial planning per se, which I would begin to perceive as a preteen in rural South Africa, nor in the gated communities that I would later discover as a student in the city; but, looking back, the lines of separation in Swaziland were just as clear as those of apartheid South Africa.

The imposing manse in which we grew up stood in stark contrast to the very modest neighboring houses. It was a concrete structure rising eight or ten meters above the ground, with long corridors and full-height windows, large balconies outside every room, and enough space around the house to host the neighborhood soccer field—if we wanted. Around it, gravel roads of a 1980s small town and neat, single-story homes made up the neighborhood. That was just the way it was.

The obvious economic inequality was not all. Despite our idyllic freedom of movement, which at times included passing through the private properties of black neighbors, to get to the places where we wanted to play, there was an unwritten rule: the manse yard was not to be entered by the children from the neighborhood. Not that I recall this ever being policed. That, too, was just the way it was. The boundaries of "white space" were to be strictly maintained, and only crossed with explicit permission, while boundaries were much more porous in many other parts of the community. Despite levels of racial integration that were taboo and legislatively forbidden just fifteen kilometers away on the other side of the border, we nonetheless reproduced the social and spatial logic of colonial racial hierarchy.

I distinctly remember one moment of conversion. I was fifteen going on sixteen, a committed evangelist who was participating in follow-up to the altar call at a church in another province. My grandfather had passed away earlier that day, but my evangelistic commitments prompted me to proceed with the church rhythms as planned, despite this loss. My grief certainly contributed to deeper receptivity on my part that day. The irony of the white evangelist conversing with a black "convert," only to undergo his own "conversion," may have become a missionary stereotype, but this instance deserves retelling.

Our ministry that night was to a sixteen-year-old congregant named Thandeka, who had responded to the altar call during worship the previous Sunday. We felt awkwardness as white missionaries entering a black home, just as the final reports of the Truth and Reconciliation Commission were being handed over to President Nelson Mandela, and the felt imbalance in power relations was difficult to put into words. Add to this two sixteen-year-old bodies, white male and black female, observed by white mentors and black family members, conversing around the age-old story of salvation, and the fact that any relationships formed at all is a wonder on its own. The "evangelism" that was taking place began as Thandeka explained that no evangelism was required—her faith was deep-rooted and her response to the altar call was a mere recommitment—and ended in a silent realization that it was I who needed conversion.

Our conversation followed paths far more mundane than the complexities of the story of salvation and community, yet what resulted was more wholesome than faith reduced to an altar call. The exact moment of my conversion was impossible to identify then, and looking back across all these years, it is even less clear now what evoked my transformation. I returned home horrified by my recognition that, despite the seeming diversity of my community, that moment was the first time I really saw a black person as my equal, as someone who shared passions and dreams and fears. It was the first time that I really grieved what apartheid had done to me.

These threads seem to be entangled in ways that will require a lifetime to unravel. There is the current promise of bodily integrity for self and loved ones that was inconceivable for previous generations, for whom our life expectancy would have resembled the stuff of science fiction, and simultaneously, a sense that just around the corner the end of the world may occur. There is a growing recognition that the world our forebears handed to us has disrupted our lives at the most intimate level, and that we will spend our lifetimes slowly working to repair the disruption, only to hand over this task and vocation to our children and grandchildren.

This is the slow work of faith that the contemporary world—a distracted world that jumps from object to object, always finding one more thing that needs attention—has little place to explore. *Is that part of our curse—a society where there are always more things that need attention? Is never stopping and always moving on to the next distraction part of how we, or I, cope?*

Importantly, there are injustices that cannot be "fixed." Our "time that has been ruined by injustice," which Silakhe Singata writes about,[6] with its woundedness, can only be grieved with sorrow that requires our stopping. Taking note. Just sitting with it. Perhaps this is the biggest lesson I take from looking back on this first part of my life. I have become more fully aware of what will not be fixed. That which needs to be grieved. The loss that needs to be allowed to become part of us, to change how we see life.

JESUS AND JUSTICE

On the whole we don't take Jesus seriously.

ALBERT NOLAN[7]

6. Following John D. Caputo but also bringing the language of ruined time, of things that cannot be "fixed," into the world, which I also need to inhabit. Singata, "Justice for the Dead," 323.

7. Nolan, *Jesus Today*, xvii.

Kerke preek nooit oor werk, politiek, seks, of geld nie. Wat is daar dan nog oor om oor te preek?

ETIENNE DE VILLIERS[8]

In a way, my years of theological study and years of academic theological work seem to remain a long-winded attempt at responding to the question I grappled with as a teenager: *What would Jesus do?* That was my generation. We wore WWJD bracelets directing our faith towards ethics, of sorts, and then I simultaneously found myself wrestling with the critical theological questions of who this Jesus really was, on the one hand, and on the other hand, what it meant to face my whiteness in the aftermath of apartheid.

The nagging suspicion throughout this social and theological quest has been that Nolan was right. We don't take Jesus seriously. But more than that, this taking seriously should find its place not primarily in the withdrawn moments of spiritual discernment, but in everyday life. On the one hand, I look at Sunnyside, near Pretoria's city center, where I live, and at the scars left—in part by white flight, capital flight, and instability—as the city has transitioned from the apartheid era, and I wonder about so many white Christians, and why their faith could not serve as a resource to bond them with this place when social forces tempted so many to believe that it was time for white people to leave.

On the other hand, I see the scars in the South African psyche brought about by the blatant display of wealth in a country of immense poverty. *Does our faith provide resources that we need to stop perpetuating our uniquely South African version of suburban sprawl and spatial inequality?* Apartheid's spatial vision separated us in terms of how material welfare corresponded with racial grouping. In the afterlife of apartheid, the gated community as the ultimate vision of the good life continues to haunt our cities as they struggle

8. "Churches never preach about work, politics, sex, or money. What is there left then to preach about?" Quoted from the memory of conversations we had as theological students between 2006 and 2012.

to achieve a common good—the good that really is common to all.[9]

Jim Perkinson's words continue to resonate with me:

> What if salvation actually is all about salvation, that is to say, that there indeed is no wholeness at any level without wholeness at every level? What if, in fact, we are interlinked in such a way that the first world cannot become healthy without the two-thirds world also becoming healthy? Not as a matter of prescription, but as simple description?[10]

What if the city won't find peace until the township finds wholeness? What if the wholeness of the margins really is tied up with the wholeness of the city . . . as one whole? If the call truly is about salvation that touches all, how might I hear this very personal call on my own life?

This tugging at the heart, right from my childhood searching, has been about what it means to really follow this Jesus.

During my years of theological study and early ministry, it was that brief phrase that Jesus spoke to those who would become disciples that often prompted my reflections: *Follow me.* These simple words captured my own call to ministry and underpinned core decisions in my life. *Follow me.* Yes, working out the following is a lifelong journey. *But is that not in part why we continue to be drawn to this Jesus?* On the one hand, the call is so simple, while on the other, there is a lifetime of being drawn deeper into its meaning. But for me, relating to this Jesus always happened from the side. The long and complicated debates on Christology from above, or below, could never really encapsulate to me how Jesus relates to all of life. The insights of metaphysical reflection or historical research on the life of Jesus could not provide me a final word—although both were profoundly important in different ways. I know Jesus through the witness of those who walked alongside him. Jesus seen from the side.[11]

9. Van Wyngaard and Louw, "Theology from the Suburbs," 514.

10. Perkinson, "Like a Thief," 520.

11. Van Aarde, *Fatherless in Galilee*, 13–14.

Those who speak of his divinity often seem to know too much, with their literal, God's-eye view, of how the God-human Christ "works." *How do they assume to know this?* I often wonder. Strangely, those who seem to be able to reconstruct, in the minutest detail, the humanity of this person—his personality and style, and even the most intimate possibilities of sexuality or desire—seem also to assume too much in understanding a person from antiquity, apparently with more clarity than I have about myself. Yes, I admit to employing caricature. My aim is to highlight the unique perspective of seeing Jesus from the side, through the eyes of those who follow. My search has been one of listening to those who shared what they experienced, who wrote down what they heard, as *those who walked alongside.* While not blind to their embellishments, I could not disregard their experiences. Most importantly, mine has been a search to learn from those who took up these words and crafted a way of life from them, over centuries.

Does this mean that Jesus is mostly an ethical guide? I refuse the reduction, but there is something in seeing Jesus exactly as ethical guide that I want to embrace. For me, Jesus is indeed primarily about how I live. And Jim Perkinson's words that have been ringing in the back of my mind for so many years, focus this: "There is only the way one lives, and what one lives for."[12] Thus, Jesus is about how I look at the world around me, how I relate to the people around me, and how I place myself in this world. Even while engaging questions that Jesus, the Jesus I know from the side, couldn't have imagined, I still find myself pondering, *What would Jesus have done with my questions? Or rather: if our paths have crossed, and if he called me from that tree and we had a meal, what would he have had me do?*

Over the years this thought has engineered its way into my convictions: that if we are to take Jesus seriously, then it must be visible in the lives we live. Not the lives we want to live, or the lives we live after hours, when we close the office door or before our children return from school, but in the actual lives we live, all our days—a simple life that reduces the resources we are dependent

12. Perkinson, *White Theology*, 215.

on, seeking the repair of all the earth. It must be visible whether we throw our weight behind the politics that will ensure the material well-being of those most vulnerable today or live in ways that refuse a blatant display of wealth in the face of immense poverty. It might be visible in the choice of the place that we work to make our home, or in the people to whom we commit and call our community. Or, sometimes, in merely insisting on treating neighbors and strangers with decency, or in moments where we truly gift the smallest part of what we have to those we are intimately bound to—with no expectation of recognition or reciprocity.

Our quest for justice must draw on the wisdom of the best social, economic, and political analyses, in the hope that our choices and actions will mirror the justice that Jesus and our faith call us to. In addition, our faith in Jesus must embrace the tension between aligning with big agendas that create the welfare of all and exercising our most intimate choices—whom we live with, the community that we call our own, and the ways in which we raise our children—if our faith is to take Jesus seriously.

By living into this integrity, between my most intimate life and my public commitments, the answer of my adolescent grappling with what Jesus would do has begun to emerge.

BECOMING WHOLE

Russel Botman shares the now famous story of the University of the Western Cape Systematic Theology class taught by Jaap Durand, where Durand drew from his students an answer to the question: "Why is apartheid a *theological* problem?" Their reply was that apartheid assumes the inherent irreconcilability of people—thus refusing the reconciling work of Christ.[13] Their conclusions were not the last words on this matter. For example, a few years later, David Bosch unpacked the conviction that apartheid is "nothing but a heresy" by focusing on how a distorted understanding of the church, of Christian community, underpinned this political

13. Botman, "Barmen to Belhar."

system;[14] and Simon Maimela described the anthropological heresy underpinning apartheid, because apartheid refused to see the inherent goodness in God's creation, of all people![15]

Closer to my meditation here, Murray Coetzee describes apartheid as a quasi-soteriology.[16] It is a distorted vision of wholeness, where salvation is found in separation. Apartheid is the logical conclusion of centuries of colonial and modern Christian reflection, where holiness and purity find an ironic synonymity. Being holy, being righteous, and being dedicated to God are equated with ideas around purity that can only be realized when being cut off from parts of the world; holiness quite literally conflated "racial purity" with convictions of "being saved." The irony in this "soteriology" is obvious when we discover Jesus on the outside of this system of Christian thought, given Jesus' complete disregard for systems of purity in the gospels. Nevertheless, a soteriology that equates holiness and purity has been the norm rather than the exception in the history of the Christian faith. Yet the very fact that we find this distorted logic so blatantly expressed in the faith of the apartheid churches should act as a warning and a sign that our past struggles against apartheid Christianity might yet be required as an antibody for this persisting, toxic, quasi-soteriology in our churches and our society. If our vision of holiness requires a commitment to purity, that divides us from other people and the world in which we live, then there are very real risks that we may step into a quest for salvation that cannot commit to God's quest to save all of creation.

I sometimes fear that our desire for holiness has morphed into a deep hate of people. Perhaps that is too strong. It's just that people are considered an obstacle to holiness. Wholeness is sold with imagery of gently flowing streams, sunsets over empty beaches, or silent forest walks. Christians explore Jesus' withdrawals to mountains as exemplary for our lives. *But what about the crowds pushing from all sides? What about the touch that draws*

14. Bosch, "Nothing but a Heresy."

15. Maimela, "Anthropological Heresy."

16. Coetzee, *"Kritiese Stem" teen Apratheidsteologie*, 35.

power and makes whole? What about the wounded appearance that brings healing? In a world of eight billion people, how do we find wholeness in the noise? Not in moments of withdrawal, but in the embrace, the gentle touch of a stranger, the clustering around of loved ones.

Put a few people together, and quickly wholeness emerges as something that is constructed. Something found. Something about which different eyes illuminate different dimensions. Not an ancient fixedness to just return to, but an ever-elusive possibility, somewhere in the future. Allow us to sit around deeper into the night, and you will find that my wholeness is tied with yours. Merely insisting on what I desire when this desire may cause pain to another does not bring wholeness to either of us. The wholeness that calls from the future must bring wholeness not only for me but for us.

Wholeness then becomes something tentative. Something found momentarily, then evading us again. Ever disrupted by another. Ever dependent on another. Not pushed off to the new heaven and earth. Not assured by a single comfort in life or death. But a possibility that emerges from the risk of living with people. Not as a guarantee, but as a possibility, on the other side of loving and allowing myself to be loved.

Again, I write from a particular place, in urban South Africa, my earphones playing soothing repetitive sounds that drown out the city noises for a moment on a Sunday afternoon. It's a street I know. The place that has been called home for the longest single period of my life. The only place my children have ever called home. When I name the place to those familiar with the dynamics of the city, the name Sunnyside immediately evokes a response. It's not just another place. People share a bank of emotions and expectations about these streets. Given the nature of housing in this part of the city, its proximity to multiple universities, and easy access to public transport, many people share a story of living here at some point—usually briefly, and usually during the formative time of early adulthood. This was home for the season of tertiary studies, or during that first employment. It carries memories. But even more, today it calls up visceral responses of fear and confusion—possibly like inner-city areas elsewhere. Is it safe? Do you have children? And sometimes just the instinctive "why?" Why is this the place you call home?

Exploring the "why" would require recounting our journey through attempts at sustainable urban living—in smaller circles of movement where the greater parts of our daily routines are shared, and in finding ways to disrupt the reproduction of apartheid spatial design and relational ties. But the truth is that at some point our initial explorations faded somewhat, and what remains is simply that this is the place that became home. Each physical landmark carries a memory, and life was woven into layers of networks that keep the heartbeat of this community alive. So, as noises continue on the other side of these earphones, drifting indoors from some gathering that no doubt breaks a slew of bylaws—a gathering most likely attended by those who drove into the neighborhood because of the blind eye that law enforcement turns to inner cities, often to the detriment of the communities that stay here—I allow myself to become increasingly conscious of where it is that I'm thinking from.

It is against this background that I am trying to make sense of our search for wholeness, from within the noisiness of inner cities that have fallen out of favor, inner cities abandoned for gated communities and new business districts, leaving metropolitan areas that are "too big to fail"[17] and that seem to be increasingly out of step with a healthy city's rhythm. Out of step, because in all the attempts to carve out small parts of our cities that can be portrayed as good, the walls, electric fences, and endless security guards remind us that our cities are not whole.

Yet, exactly in this absence of purity, in this place where we rub shoulders across nationalities, where household surveys find people across vastly different income levels living as neighbors, where law enforcement and private security companies accept (albeit grudgingly) the coexistence of homeless communities alongside more settled neighbors, and where every so often, the

17. Haffagee, "Joburg Is Too Big."

community of sex workers and the community of faith overlap—exactly in this place, where the myth of purity is exposed for the absurdity that it is and has always been, something of the holy might be traced.

I make no romantic claims about urban South Africa. Rubbing shoulders comes with friction, and economically diverse communities do not coexist with a promise of resources being shared—at least not very often. Merely making peace with living among those who have fallen outside the structures of modern society does not equate with a posture of hospitality. Perhaps more than anything, rooting down in this place refuses the salvific myths that have informed much of modern life: those where withdrawal and cutting ourselves off from those who are different promises wholeness—a wholeness for some that is conditioned on disconnecting from the very whole of the One who is named creator of all. I live with this nagging suspicion that only when the myth of purity is shattered will we have the possibility of discovering the wholeness of a salvation that "actually is all about salvation,"[18] and the sounds around me are constant reminder that right here lies the possibility we are searching for.

TOWARDS A LIFE LIVED

I could not have imagined that an invitation to explore faith through this act of writing, reflecting on the brief vignettes of a life lived, would return me to the mundane place of middle life. Writings about Jesus and justice often evoke accounts of near heroic feats of world-changing disruption. Raising children and paying bills seldom remind of such heroism.

However, the life ordinarily lived is exactly where we should go. Not just in reference to my midlife experiences written up here, per se, but in the mundaneness of doing all of our lives *with people*. Daily. Simply. Allowing life's fullness to be intertwined with others. *How does life become whole in the midst of the mundane?* At heart,

18. Perkinson, *White Theology*, 217.

it is about discovering that faith and following Jesus find their place in the daily rhythms of life. In our world, nearly everything has been reduced to an economic quest for keeping poverty and unemployment at bay, perhaps most visibly in the ways in which we too often begrudge rather than cherish our life's work and our labors, and large parts of our waking lives are only grudgingly accepted and often experienced as generally meaningless.[19] On the contrary, our labor can become our spiritual practice. Building. Forming. *Why can our faith not tell us when to quit a task or job? Why does our faith so seldom direct us to what we should do, or how to approach what we do? Is it still possible to develop a faith-filled imagination, freed from economic calculations, that irresistibly draws our hands and minds to what can only be named as calling?*

> Why is it that we remain unable to present a Christian vision of concrete life together that may be a captivating alternative to the scars of separation that mark contemporary urban designs? Why is it that our faith too often cannot meaningfully speak to the most important decision of our lives: Where we will put down roots? Where will home be?[20]

Other than emigration and semigration, there is the gravitational pull of the pure and pristine gated community—promising salvation for some—or just the estate agent's mantra: *location, location, location*. Little can form us more deeply than deciding on where we will live. If the faith we are called to is about the whole of life, then surely it must touch ground exactly in this question—rooting us in ways that will direct the way we live.

Obviously, everything I suggest here is defined by the possibility of choice. That choices can be made about the places we call home or the labor we call employment. For many that possibility of choice remains elusive. That we live in a world where the majority of people have no choice in where they live or work should not escape our attention. Because the Gospel stories of call and response—of Jesus' words and the reorientation of disciples'

19. Graeber, *Bullshit Jobs*.

20. Van Wyngaard and Louw, "Theology from the Suburbs," 495.

lives—that have captivated the community of faith over centuries imply both a choice and a reordering of our world in ways that make choice possible. That is, possible for all. *What might our world become if everyone had agency concerning the places they called "home" and the hours of their lives that are described as "work"? As impossible as it seems, near the southern tip of Africa, what might it mean to live life in ways that will birth such a possibility for the people whose lives touch ours?*

As I look back on my life lived thus far, from zealous teenage commitments, maturing into professional theological convictions, I tend to circle back to the life choices that inform my most mundane of moments. *With whom am I to be in community? Where will I put down roots? What will I commit to spend my energy on?*

A LAST WORD ON GRIEF

There were many moments in penning words about faith across these pages, when this word "grief" caused writer's block. One aspect of the stereotypical midlife crisis, which those who are younger detest, with reason, is recognizing that there are things that won't be repaired in our lifetimes. There are parts of our life together that have been ruined beyond repair. *How do we grieve for a world that could have been but that will not ever be? How do we grieve in ways that draw us towards working for what might still be, nonetheless?*

Once, when I was a young student minister, a wise elder, on hearing what my postgraduate area of focus was, asked, "How long will we still have to deal with it?"—"it" here referring to questions of racism in South Africa. Without thinking, I answered, "Three generations of hard work, and yet we are still not working very hard at this, at the moment." Much has changed in our political landscape since that day, and what was silent back then has frequently been loudly engaged in our public debates in the past decade. But in the process, we have learned just how deeply cut are the crafted distortions of our colonized world within the societies it has cut apart.

My students today speak in pessimistic modes of an antiblack world that will not change—a world fundamentally antiblack. A part of me wants to push back. I want to join the optimistic politicians who announce that change will come with the next administration, or the youth pastors who say that change will come with the next generation. I lack the certainty for using words such as "never"—history teaches us that never is a very long time—but I sit at my transition into midlife, and I have to face the fact that some things won't change in my lifetime.

The challenge of faith, then, seems to be to learn to grieve for a world that will not be, to interrupt any cynical acceptance of prevalent evil and injustice in the world, and to live ordinary lives in ways that anticipate and birth the impossible possibilities that are coming. Faith is found in the most mundane of choices—how we pursue meaning in tasks or work, how we say no to meaningless promotions, how we accompany our children in committing to a life that makes room for the impure and to a community that sometimes fits like a knobbly chair: although uncomfortable, it always prods us to shift and make room for living with people in ever-broadening ways.

CHAPTER TWO

Just | Grief | Whole

Laurie Gaum

When a white, English-speaking male South African asked four white, Afrikaner males to write on such an evocative theme as ours, I was skeptical along with the others. *What would we have to say? Do we have anything to contribute? Would there be readers like you interested in our stories?* I became more intrigued as the project progressed, in online meetings and a writers' retreat, which got relocated to Pretoria. There, an idea started to emerge for me to write a vignette connected to each theme—each as a lens for self-reflection. So, I brought incidents to mind that defined each theme for me—incidents that in the end have defined me. Narrating this is what follows. Readers might notice that at times there is no clear demarcation between justice, grief, and wholeness. Sometimes the one may be more about the other. But perhaps they form a weave, of one threaded into the other, the wholeness coming through grief, always on the spoor of justice.

JUST | GRIEF | WHOLE

South Africa was busy awakening from its apartheid sleep when I began my studies in theology. This was the early nineties at the University of Stellenbosch near Cape Town. Stellenbosch was the intellectual cradle in which apartheid ideology was born. I was born into the Dutch Reformed Church (DRC) in Wellington. My lineage already included a grandfather on my mother's side who was a DRC minister, as well as an uncle in the ministry, his son just having completed his theological studies. Furthermore, I was in training for Dutch Reformed ministry, following in my father's footsteps, who was in the leadership of the church as editor of its official newspaper, *Kerkbode*, and as secretary of its General Assembly.

The first struggle in my life must have been with my father. The decision about theology was difficult for me, between pursuing a more creative occupation like architecture and a more people-centered one, like theology. Theology was supposedly about the most significant things in life, about God. It had *significance* written all over it. But to be *called* to it seemed essential. And I was grappling with this vocation business—how authentic this calling was for me. Architecture, I then argued, was a more masculine and therefore more *acceptable* art form to explore, for a man. But this, I feared, would mean opting out of engaging with the Divine and would easily land me without faith.

As young, white Afrikaners and future DRC ministers in formation, many of us were actively engaging with the legacy of apartheid, and with the church we would become ministers to, which had legitimized the apartheid ideology, scripturally.

The country was opening up to democracy on various fronts after the unbanning of the liberation movements and the release of Nelson Mandela, during the buildup to the first democratic elections. It was a time of great possibility as leaders were returning from exile, and somehow everything was up for reorientation. We were confronted with all kinds of "awakenings." There were seven women in our class who were only allowed into full-time ministry in the DRC in the year we started our studies, 1990. They were still living in hope in October that year, when a church General Assembly decision would fully affirm their calling. A few of these women were making a considerable impact on the class and seminary. Some of my fellow male classmates, along with some male lecturers, struggled to engage with them and to accommodate and accept them as fellow theologians and future colleagues in ministry, and these men were making the women feel this.

As critical and idealistic students, some of us were deconstructing our Christian nationalist upbringing and faith background. We had to resist the old order, good heavens! Where did it land us? As the pariah of the world. This meant our educational foundations, our family lives, and our religious formation seemed compromised. I saw my father as symbolizing this old order.

How could I disagree with him and simultaneously love him? The somewhat enlightened Stellenbosch environment seemed to demand that I distance myself from his moderate, and at times conservative, voice, which was prominent in Afrikaner society.

Being on the progressive side of the class along with most of the women, many of whom were friends, meant I vicariously experienced the pain inflicted on them. Thus, I started to understand what solidarity felt like, I guess, and it was difficult. To paraphrase Dietrich Bonhoeffer, solidarity demands putting oneself at the same risk as the victim of injustice and discrimination.[1] At times, I shied away from the radicality of this solidarity, while also not completely sharing the women's experience, nor understanding it fully. But I used the values of fairness and equality, for which I had an early affinity, as a guiding principle to order and make sense of life and reality.

The formation of my theological identity took place during this time of "rainbowism." And the rainbow as an LGBTQI symbol was already heralding the hope of also encompassing "queer" identities. Later, I would learn that the first Pride march held in 1990 in South Africa, fresh after the dawn of the new dispensation, would have as its theme "A Queer South Africa." For me, more personal awakenings were in the process of unfolding. But this would be co-determined by my women friends and colleagues in their struggle to be treated justly. This common affinity would, however, also soon mean that I would more intimately experience an exclusion echoing theirs, as prejudice impacted on my own skin. But

1. Bonhoeffer, *Cost of Discipleship*, 97.

speaking of skin, which has defined our country for centuries, there's another defining moment in my story that comes to mind, which led me into the "valley of death."

JUST | **GRIEF** | WHOLE

I gradually grew into a calling and into ministry. Especially into the practical side. I didn't see much sense in too cerebral and abstract a study of theology, although I liked philosophy. I should have continued with postgraduate philosophy but retreated from it for a similar reason to why I shied away from architecture, namely, that too much thought would end up as an irresistible temptation to my faith. *Or was it because there was another shadow lurking?*

I had the usual evangelical awakening at Stellenbosch, being passionate about Christ in every sense, but in a very personalized and pious way. I was impressed by the revival movements in Holland, Britain, and North America that we studied in church history, and that, from the nineteenth century, also became hugely influential in the DRC, through figures like Andrew Murray Jr.

But for me, there was a social and contextual emphasis that was beginning to emerge. I became part of an outreach action group at the DRC student congregation, or Student Church, on campus, visiting the newest, sprawling black township outside Cape Town—Khayelitsha. We were naively going to the township to do door-to-door evangelization. I was simultaneously a frequent visitor to the Stellenbosch township, Khayamandi, building friendships there and beginning to taste the magic of township energy. I was also aware of an overwhelming sense of dread at the scale of poverty.

After completing my studies at the seminary, and with my evangelical zeal still more or less in place, I opted to do the denomination's service year for Christ. There was a sense of adventure attached to this as we would go as a team of young people to Belgium for nine months, participating in a door-to-door evangelization campaign. I knew Belgium was largely a Catholic country, but we were determined to bring the evangelical gospel to this culturally religious nation. We stayed on barges, moving from place to place in Flemish-speaking Flanders, and I had a few good conversations with a younger Catholic priest. I also had some clashes with the South African leadership of our outreach by supposedly asking too many questions.

During the time overseas, I wrote a letter back home to my parents telling them I would not seek the usual route of congregational ministry, which they were envisioning for me, but rather an alternative one of community involvement, perhaps in a black congregation, to familiarize myself better with a South African context that I was not yet well exposed to. I had, after all, grown up in the average "protected," white, Afrikaans "bubble" in Wellington, where the rumblings of a frustrated South Africa were only sounding far off on the fringes of our awareness. I followed news from abroad as the Truth and Reconciliation Commission's work was unfolding and was fascinated with it since I had focused my final year thesis at Stellenbosch on the development of transitional church rituals for South Africa's political transition.

My father was instrumental through his network in hearing of an option for me to serve as assistant minister in a Presbyterian church in Gugulethu, another black township of Cape Town. The minister of this congregation, Spiwo Xapile, was visionary in many ways, and, after having had an American woman pastor in the assistant minister role, saw fit to extend the position to a young, inexperienced, white Afrikaner male. Amy Biehl, the well-known American Fulbright scholar, was murdered only four years earlier (1993), in NY1, the main arterial road of this apartheid-designed township. A few hundred meters down NY1 from the humble cross marking Amy's death, a memorial would be built for the Gugulethu Seven, killed in 1986 by the South African Police.

But now was a different time. South Africa's Rainbow Nation was in full emergence. There was hope in the air. Everything was possible. Everything was open for reinvention. Our world-leading constitution, hailed for its progressivity, was just finalized and endorsed. The then–deputy president, Thabo Mbeki, had made his epic "I am an African" speech at the tabling of the constitution. We had to catch up to the world at an accelerating pace regarding race, gender, sexual orientation, and the need for social development. South Africa's awakening was indeed in full swing.

Since my appointment followed that of a white, American, woman pastor, and the congregation was quite used to many (white) overseas visitors, I could move into her slipstream and get along without too many challenges to my social background and my relation to South African history. I had to find my feet in a very demanding and, for me, strange context, although I was just twenty kilometers away from my parental home in the posh Capetonian suburb of Oranjezicht where I still resided. In addition, through my Dutch Reformed connection, we learned that I was to be called by the Student Church congregation in Stellenbosch together with my placement in this Gugulethu Presbyterian congregation, the JL Zwane Memorial Church.

Thus, I was now navigating living between the cushioned spaces of Stellenbosch and Cape Town coffee shops, and the harsh realities of many poor, black South Africans. Through Spiwo's leadership, the JL Zwane congregation was engaging the challenges of the new South Africa on all fronts, creating a development center to train and provide job opportunities for unemployed youth. The church also identified the need for after-school support for learners who, in the new dispensation, accessed previously white Model C Schools, and whose parents were unable to assist them with homework. Spiwo was also exploring very innovative church-corporate partnerships to make these initiatives possible and bring immediate relief where need be.

I was doing home visitations to the elderly and sick, serving them *umthendeleko* (communion), and thus going into the homes and shacks of congregants. In addition, this meant I was getting around the township, experiencing how the apartheid spatial planning of black townships intended to limit access and maximize security control, and witnessing what this did to the sense of place and community of a horseshoe-shaped neighborhood, with its semidetached "train houses" positioned in the middle of each yard. Spiwo had a "deep end" approach, allowing me to learn firsthand. I was leading the Sunday school and was involved with the youth group. Later, we would start a junior youth group with a soccer team, and on the girls' demand also a choir. We got Stellenbosch students involved in volunteering and did a few communal camps with Gugulethu youth, sleeping over in shacks and holding storytelling sessions.

My preaching opportunities in white Dutch Reformed congregations became fewer as my sermons became more contextual. I struggled to reconcile the stark contradictions between the different worlds I was inhabiting. While I enjoyed, somehow needed, and flourished in the "coffee shop culture" of Stellenbosch and Cape Town, with its creative stimulation, another reality hit hard in the township as I was confronted with unemployment and searing poverty. I felt, like other times later in life, that I at least had the opportunity to contribute and make a difference, addressing the ills of the past that my ancestors were part of creating, the fruit of which I was enjoying. I felt that I could not distance myself from this painful past but should take responsibility for dealing with the shame and guilt that comes with it.

I had opportunities to lead funeral services and church services, struggling with my inability to get a grip on the language and the strangeness of the culture, but being led by a patient elder who accompanied me on home visitations. I was keenly dependent on young people who became friends to introduce me to, and guide me into, their world. I spent hours and hours in church services, not having a full grip of the language or meanings of the ritual dancing and praying, learning to move along with a Madiba-jive—so many hours that at times, I forgot that my skin was the lightest amid a wave of rhythms. I tried to figure out when to anticipate a chorus erupting in the middle of a sermon. My lips were struggling to get accustomed to form the names that I read off coffins at funerals.

At some stage, the funerals became more frequent. I felt drawn to become involved with the HIV and AIDS pandemic that was suddenly beginning to surface in South Africa. I am not sure when it had hit the ground in the township, nor can I remember when I became aware of it. But there was talk and energy for a coordinated response starting to develop, especially from the health sector, and a need for church involvement was also mentioned. It felt quite covert for me, but in a strange way it was energizing to attend meetings at the Triangle Project, an LGBTQI+ organization then having an office in Gugulethu.

Of course, something deeper rang true within me, so I intended to continue following this lead. I had to do a visitation to serve communion at Mother Theresa's order—the Missionaries of Charity in Khayelitsha. I felt enthralled, in the same way as I often felt in the township, by the surprises one stumbles across, when I saw the nuns in their familiar white-and-light-blue-striped garb, making their way between the sick. It echoed that strange, almost eerie, invigorating experience I had had, witnessing a goat being slaughtered on Maundy Thursday in preparation for Easter. Or when I had visited my fellow Sunday schoolteacher friend, outside his hut "in the bush" for his initiation, white clay painted on his torso. Or drinking *umqombhoti* (African traditional beer) at the home of another youth member returning from the bush. Time seemed to come to a standstill, or at least started to move slowly, as if tapping into another reality. It felt close to the pulse of life itself.

It must have been the first time I came in touch with someone on the cusp of death, clearly going to leave life in the next few hours. I was thinking of the mini thesis on rites of passage I had written. *Could a simple prayer be enough, now?* I was glad I had got the *umthendeleko* equipment with me.

The trustworthy, gray-haired and frail elder, Silimela, accompanying me through the township and to hospital, was there as always, with words to assist my lack of language. It was also the first time I came into contact with the inflamed skin of a person with full blown AIDS. I cannot remember how early it was into the pandemic or how familiar we were with protocols at the time, but I know these new experiences contributed to the severity of the moment, the sense of awe in the air. Under some sheets on the bed was not much more than bones and the transparent skin of a person. There was not much to be heard, except the sound of groans.

Somehow, I remember on the same day elsewhere in the township, around another corner, a public display of dance breaking out. I was more than captivated. It was as if I was caught unaware in the anomalies of our country, between suffering and celebration, disbelief and despair. I was trying to balance myself on the sharp edge of our nation, in the not-so-new South Africa, within our deeply broken and excruciatingly beautiful continent, Africa. I was learning profound things: basically, how life puts contrasting things together. It wasn't simple. One had to get to grips with the thorniness of life and go with the flow, accepting what is offered to you, to make the best out of it, even transforming what feels bad into what can be good. At the time, it seemed that God's strength enabled one to do this. Later, I would not be so interested anymore in the origins of things, that they needed to come from God, or anywhere else. This meant I needn't have to apportion blame so directly, to any originator. But all this still needed to come closer to home, for myself.

JUST | GRIEF | **WHOLE**

My thirty-fourth birthday coincided with Ash Wednesday. I was excited by the liturgical renewal taking place in the Dutch Reformed Church in which I was minister. I was now serving my second congregation, this time in Cape Town's inner city. St. Stephen's is unique to our denomination as it is named after a saint. According to lore, when the first theater building in Africa, in which the church was originally housed, became a church for freed slaves, it was stoned by aggrieved citizens in early Cape Town. This gave St. Stephen's its patron's name, for having long been the only congregation of color in the DRC. Most congregants were later forcibly removed from their homes in District Six under apartheid during the 1950s and 1960s.

During my four years in the congregation, I introduced an Ash Wednesday service. Being Protestant, Reformed, and Calvinist, we were thin on ritual and symbols, and it was argued that it is here where renewal lay for an overly rational church tradition.

I was sourcing the ashes from St. George's Cathedral around the corner, since I was uncertain about how to produce them.

Some weeks before my birthday, our church council voted to finally do away with one silver cup during communion, in favor of individual glasses. While I was strongly motivating for the change, thinking of practicalities, as the congregation was showing potential for growth as a racially diverse community, I wavered at the last moment, arguing that fragmenting the single cup into manifold pieces did not help at a time when the denomination was desperately yearning to display greater church unity. The council however would not stand for their dominee's doubtful spirit and gave the green light for the use of glasses.

With the Ash Wednesday service, I saw the opportunity to call the congregation forward during communion, to dispense the wine directly from the minister's single cup, taking care of sanitization issues myself. Earlier, I had gotten into trouble with the *kerkraad* (the church council) for allowing non-ordained *proponente* (trained ministers without a congregation) to serve communion. I felt they were often excluded because of discrimination, especially against women in ministry in the church, and that these prescriptions were just gatekeeping for all kinds of reasons.

For this Ash Wednesday service, I was preoccupied. Not only was it my birthday, but something else was prominent on my mind that had been shadowing me for a very long time, at least since I was six or seven years old. As a young boy it was only a vague sensibility to me, not having a name for it. The ash crosses I would administer on congregants' foreheads now signified a new point of integration towards which the arc of my life was bending.

My ministry to this conservative congregation and the same-sex relationship I was in for the first time, needed to be reconciled. I always wondered how this would happen. *Would I also end up on the front page of the tabloid press in my coming out process as often happened, or how would it go? Was that the only way?*

What a process it was, as I would later read in an article, "Struggles of Authenticity," in a wonderful book called *Performing*

Queer.[2] Coming out is a conscious process that needs to be managed strategically. It happens within a certain context and through the building of relationships.

It should preferably not be forced onto you. If one took time over many years to come to terms with and acceptance of one's identity, people should also be allowed time to come around to a new understanding of you. Sometimes it is to emerge from shame, depression, and struggle to be able to say, "This is me. This I believe. This I do." Sometimes the shame can serve as motivation towards a more authentic life.

So, I decided to invite my friends to the Ash Wednesday service, a service so emblematic of my own life. Afterwards we would go to a bar to lift a glass. The irony would not escape me regarding a poem inspired many years ago by the drinking that went on in the "stores" in the basement of the old St. Stephen's building, while the Spirit above was supposedly one of a different kind. In my time at St. Stephen's, we started a big restoration project of the building, with the basement stores being converted into small shops, one being called Saints—a very trendy drinking hole.

During the restoration project for which we had to raise several million rand, we had a few innovative fundraising projects, partnering with *Die Burger* newspaper. St. Stephen's appointed a theater-master, and we staged several productions. I was energized by experimenting with "inner city" ministry. During the restoration we started with the front façade of the building and I opted for a bright red paint finish for the front door and window frames, which the original theater had. After all the effort and millions, the building needed to look fresh. This caused rancor in the congregation with many *seeing red*. Somehow, this color choice was a reminder of all that was evil, of that time when the building was associated with ill repute. The color also cut close to the bone of what the congregation was fearing from the incumbent in their own pulpit.

Back at the Ash Wednesday service on my birthday, the liturgy flowed, and I could see the congregants connecting to the

2. Van Zyl and Steyn, *Performing Queer*, 195–233.

brokenness and vulnerability of life, and of their own lives, to the fragmented history of the city in which St. Stephen's was embedded, as an anomaly rooted in the African soil of our complex South African society. The square the building was located on was, after all, originally called African Square, later renamed Riebeeck Square.

"Remember that you are dust and to dust you shall return. Turn away from sin and believe the good news." I was addressing my gay friend as he reached the front of the aisle, and I drew the ash in cruciform on his forehead. At that time, I was reflecting on alternate meanings to the symbolism of the cross, not mainly as an instrument of torture, but echoing my experience of seeking a space for convergence at its center—a point of integration. I then dispensed the wine from my hand, from the single cup. That Ash Wednesday service became a beautiful evening, both in church with the congregation and afterwards down below, in the celebration.

April Fools' Day later that same year would coincide with me being exposed on the front page of a tabloid as being gay and in a relationship. The following Monday, my partner would die, by taking his own life.

Now, I had to deal simultaneously with loss and grief on many levels. April Fool's Day fell on a Friday that year, and on that day the *Son* newspaper, which previously only came out on a Sunday, became a daily. I was their cover story that launched that Friday. But it was not only a wordy story. The few words were accompanied by explicit pictures with captions exposing me as a fraud. In the front-page photo, I was supposedly making a mockery of my clerical calling by being caught pants down. Closer inspection would show that I was wearing my partner's leather jacket, and that the photo was taken some months earlier in Holland, where we, among other things, received a blessing on our troubled union. All of this became a further exposé for the Sunday newspaper.

Our relationship was troubled indeed. My partner had provided the supposedly compromising photos of me (some taken on a deserted beach, being in my most carefree, naked state) to my church council, to the circuit of congregations that the church belonged to, and to the *Son* and Sunday newspaper, *Rapport*. Over the next few days and weeks, these photos would slowly be released in the papers along with every bit of new information coming forward on the church case that soon followed.

First, my life was investigated by the circuit, then by the regional synod; then it was before the General Assembly of the DRC. I was suspended by the church council, and the circuit began investigating the accusations my partner leveled against me. In a state of mental aberration, he accused me of many things he was party to. But uppermost on the church agenda was: Was I gay? Was I in a gay relationship? Did I have gay sex? Was I promiscuous? Being in a gay relationship at that time, after all, meant being promiscuous! These questions were heavily debated as the press had a field day.

The Afrikaans daily *Die Burger* also traced the unfolding case and gave me a right of reply. Some days *Rapport* would report that I could not be found for comment, while I could not remember my phone ever ringing with their request. Other media outlets also covered the story. At first, I walked daily to the café near my sister's house, where I now found refuge, to read about the next installment of my life. When I first heard from a classmate minister about the story breaking on *Son*'s front page, I asked my mom for a sleeping tablet late that afternoon, before having to face up to the onslaught the next morning. It felt as if something had collapsed inside me, as everything came down, crushing.

Meanwhile, my partner had died. For a long time, I had taken a lot of meaning out of keeping him connected to life, trying to steer him away from the precipice. Soon after I met him on the steps of a church stoep (as he would often relate the story), he made a first attempt at suicide. I just did not know what to make of it. I was in my first intimate relationship and head over heels in love.

In my previous experience, it had taken me a long time to figure out who I was, to make peace with my faith, with God, with my calling. At times I had to convince myself I was at least still fighting with God. An Ignatian spiritual exercise of imaginative contemplation helped me to get to a point where I could place myself into the scene of God creating me and then listen to God's thoughts about me, also expressed in the words, "And it was good." I came to the point when I could claim for myself that I too, as gay, was created in God's image. This meant I was created gay in God's image, with everything that this truth implies. Somewhere along the line, I began understanding the Bible required a more metaphoric and symbolic reading, which made it a more invitational and dynamic dance of a text.

Next came the sharing with key friends, with my father, my mother, and my family. This was a second great struggle in my life. But it gradually led to an integration of aspects of myself into a more unified identity, with everything coherent. But it still did not mean I had much relationship experience. Then, I was having to be with someone who was clearly in pain. I could accompany him to the dark places of his life but in the process, I still had to manage my own insecurities.

The first time my lips touched his I was so surprised that a man's lips could be so soft. At first, I felt exposed to go out in public with him, but I came quickly to the realization that I could not hide my life. There was no alternative than to live it as an "open secret." So many had done it before. This meant I had to navigate in my new congregation to whom I had just become minister, along with this first romantic relationship.

Now, after Douw's death, everything had to be pieced together anew. I had to build a new life, having lost a partner, my job, and probably my career. Everything was messy. I grappled with shame and guilt attached to a suicide, on a very public platform, and how it affected family and friends. There was not much choice other than to own up to my identity and embrace myself. It being so public perhaps made it easier, with the support of so many reaching out and surrounding me. I just had to find the next step. And at the time, I expressed it as God making something good out of a mess. From the guiding light of justice and through the darkest valley of despair, I was stepping into my truth, taking up my cross, as a headline read. I was becoming whole.

Some years later, I attended a course on the American spiritual writer and mentor to Martin Luther King Jr., Howard Thurman, studying his writing during a fellowship year at an interfaith seminary in Hartford, Connecticut. Thurman's words, that "one must be at home somewhere in order to be at home everywhere,"[3] became a clarion call for my life—a journey of coming home to self to be able to reach out from there and find "home" within the wider embrace of all humanity, even with all beings. I was coming to see this as one and the same with my wholeness journey.

Consequently, how am I doing on this journey into wholeness, since it is also, in my view, a reintegration into the greater whole? Now I'm able to facilitate with colleagues the homecoming journey for others. My life has been totally redefined, although I can still see this aligned to an original *calling*. Perhaps it looks completely different and wasn't at all as I originally imagined. But I was liberated into my truth and to fully embrace it. The work I facilitate is indeed aiming to allow everyone to step into their truth, to claim the light, and to be able to engage with and verbalize their stories for themselves—to be at home somewhere in order to share it with others.

Through having sat in so many circles, speaking of my own story and listening to that of others, healing has gradually come as balm to the opened wounds, having given them air and cleansed them out in the ointment of truth telling. *Am I still hurting, experiencing pain, from the hurt inflicted on me by "the church," for its not understanding, its reacting in such a harsh way by seeking expulsion?* My understanding of others in my story grows with time, with listening, and with my own healing progress. What was especially hard for me was that when that part of my identity, which to some extent was insignificant, became public overnight, the rest of my ministry was disregarded, and I was shunned as a colleague, no longer to be considered one of the fold.

3. Thurman, *Luminous Darkness*, 34.

While I can understand that the circumstances under which the "scandal" happened were difficult for people to stomach, I was indeed the same person as the moment before, on this integrative journey to which my spiritual growth had led me. The sensationalist way in which it all came to light did not help the way it was perceived. While I could come away with only my integrity intact, as a friend observed, this very much depended on the point of view from which I was perceived. For many, it was impossible to see any further than the surface.

Some years later, I was co-facilitating a workshop with American evangelical pastors in Boston, Massachusetts. We were in a breakout group of the males in the training, speaking to our pain and suffering growing up as boys, which we still experienced now as men. Earlier in the workshop, I had already shared a bit of my story. Then a pastor working for the organization True Love Waits, promoting sexual abstinence before marriage, shared his experience of his son coming out to him a year earlier. He explained how this changed his perspective and made him shift his understanding. Others also joined in sharing their related experience.

Years before, I had been able to go to a pastoral psychologist along with my father, enabling us to thrash out my whole experience together. My father engaged firsthand with what same-sex orientation and love are all about, and we had to integrate it with our understanding of God, faith, church, and calling. But in the Boston workshop, far away from home, I was hearing it out of the mouth of an evangelical pastor who was not related to me, who was not so different from the ministers in my denomination who, I sometimes felt, persecuted me.

This experience moved me to better empathize, hopefully in greater compassion, with the position of "the other side." *Does this mean I don't become angry and frustrated anymore or feel resentful at times?* Here I don't want to minimize the rightful anger that one often feels, which at times motivates one to protest and actively seek justice. I also don't want to pretend that I'm not still petty at times, caught in my pain, and wilfully transmitting it, rather than being committed to transform it. But I suppose, I am committed to progress, to keep doing the work, to revisit my story, and to keep on reworking it.

While I was now on the margins of the church, I discovered so much new energy in the new people I encountered. This new journey I was on was meant for me to *transcend* the church. I was sad that at that time there was no accommodation by the church of where my integrative journey took me. With the risk of sounding judgmental, I feel that I have somehow outgrown the church.

As a young boy it became clear to me that "in order not to go to hell" is not a good enough reason to believe. There simply had to be more to faith than that. Therefore, this search for the deepest meaning of life led me to occupy my time and my life in this quest.

When I was based for several years at the Centre for Christian Spirituality established by Desmond Tutu in Cape Town, I reflected on the aptness of a truism that religion concerns people afraid of going to hell, while spirituality is for those who've already been there. The Thurman interfaith peace-building course in the United States also helped me to widen my perspective even further. In the absence of church, my need for community did not evaporate, and I had to translate it into other forms of community, which can be found anywhere if one simply opens one's eyes: in the neighborhood, in the art scene, among writers, in the interfaith community, on the margins. These places are where so many people reached out to me. I felt held, and there was new space for creativity.

Having been through such a trauma, things could not stay the same. Growth had to occur, and it needed to happen in different configurations. As we learned the hard way in the DRC, after our biblical legitimization of apartheid, we might also have been open about *being wrong* in other ways. We were clearly wrong about gender, relegating women to second-class citizenship along with others for centuries, just as the church was long wrong about slavery, and race as an extension of slavery. We are now waking up to the fact that we have been wrong about sexual orientation and gender identity and expression. *What else have we been wrong about in our interpretation? What else are we continuing to get wrong alongside others?* Our ability to interpret our holy text along with that of other religions is limited to our subjectivity and our limited consciousness. We have done so much damage to our vulnerable planet. As humans we are continuing to wage wars.

Our perspective is limited. *Where does this leave me regarding faith?* The image I have of God has grown considerably, first out of the confines of a laager mentality and a primitive understanding of the Divine, and then perhaps even beyond the confines of "godhood." Our contemporary understanding of sexuality and gender has grown since it was first publicly debated in the wake of the Kinsey Report in that infamous year of 1948. It is now accepted to think about same sex and opposite sex attraction in terms of a continuum. Today this also gets applied to gender in terms of the masculine and feminine, which is now understood as being fluid.

We are moving away from fixed, binary positions as if there were only ever two monolithic options. As far as faith is concerned, I would argue for thinking in a similar kind of continuum, not just between faith and doubt, but perhaps between being a believer and being a nonbeliever. I believe there are many shades of gray in between, and I do not want to be painted into a corner. I am comfortable with being mobile on such a faith continuum, sometimes not using much of a faith paradigm at all, while at other times drawing on the rich stories, rituals, disciplines, values, and wisdom of my Christian tradition. I need not express so precisely what the content of my faith, or lack of it, is. For this reason, I have at times been hesitant to put my hand to paper, to nail my colors to one mast.

After all I have narrated, how do I then see my calling or vocation? Except for being an artist at heart, and a theological or rather a spiritual activist at times, I am intent on being a healer. In this journey, I stay committed to my own healing: healing from being on the receiving end of injury, from a system of oppression and its sometimes un-self-aware agents. This oppression has not been fully transformed, often continuing to exclude and inflict pain, injustice, and discrimination. I have learned some hard lessons along the way, not having yet arrived, but continuing to learn, becoming more knowledgeable, and understanding in my encounter with the other, listening deeply to their shared experiences.

I hope I may continue to be used in the healing journey of others. Through my encounter with their pain and suffering, sitting with them as they cry, and as I sit with my own tears, I get transformed. I get cleansed by the mercy of salty water. And communally, we are embracing each other, finding that next step in the dark. The healing comes even if the journey is long. We are together in the recovery process, being made whole, finding the healing, and doing our work in community; we are reintegrating our different parts, reintegrating our lives.

Being home somewhere, I am home everywhere.

CHAPTER THREE

Walking Pathways to Wholeness

Rex van Vuuren

SOME THOUGHTS ABOUT BEGINNINGS[1]

Rex is my name. I carry my mother's family name as first name. She was a descendent of George Rex of Knysna. Legend has it, and it persists today, that George Rex was an illegitimate son of King George III.

I grew up in a very Afrikaans community where every third dog was name Rex. When aunty Susan stood in her kitchen door she would call out, "Rex! Rex!" I straightened up thinking she called me. At primary school I was often teased with snapping fingers calling, "Rex! Rex!" I became very ashamed of my name.

As a child I was brought up to own or to have strong religious beliefs—a set of propositions and a *faith* that enabled me to trust these beliefs. I believed implicitly in the existence of God. Mine was also the Protestant Reformed belief in the prospect of eternal damnation, or, as a redeemed Christian, in a heavenly life after

1. In writing this chapter I acknowledge the influence of some important mentors and colleagues on my personal and professional journey. Most importantly: Prof. J. H. van den Berg, Dutch psychiatrist and phenomenologist; Prof. Bernd Jager, Canadian psychologist and phenomenologist; Dr. Hans Bürki in his visits to the Students' Christian Association; and Prof. Dreyer Kruger, psychologist and phenomenologist of Rhodes University.

death. As I grew up, I realized that there was more to religion than a misconstrued *fear of God*. This "fear" is captured in the obsessively recurring motif of the Reformed Protestant dogma of the "people of the covenant." The center of gravity lay in the Abrahamic and later the Mosaic sealing of the covenant between God and his chosen people, the breach of the covenant, the consequences of disobedience, and then the restoration of the covenant, which seemed obligatory for the resolution of the narration of this good story.

Where I grew up, most people attended church with all the rules and expectations that made up Afrikaner middle-class society. Christian Reformed morality ordered our household. I never abandoned the traditions that supported me in my teen years. Yet, in my early twenties, I slowly became aware of the existential problems that accompany maturity. My burgeoning concern and questions about moral justice found no immediate resolution.

I received piano lessons from the age of ten to sixteen. I learnt to read music. Even now I enjoy following music through the music scores. The book of Psalms that we sang in the Reformed Church included the musical notation of each Psalm. Following the notation, I often sang the Psalms to myself, feeling their musicality, but hardly understanding the depth and reach of the meaning of the words.

I often read and sang verses such as, "Bless the Lord O my Soul!" in Ps 103. For years I tried to figure out: *What does it mean to "bless God," and what does the word "soul" refer to?* As time passed, I understood that in Christian religious terms, "Bless the Lord O my Soul!" meant, among other things, *I am telling myself to praise the Lord with all that is within me—to speak to and about the Lord in ways that bring him honor and glory*. This expresses my gratitude to the Lord for all his benefits.

Despite catechism, confirmation at the age of sixteen, Bible readings, and many sermon monologues, nothing, as far as I was aware, had yet happened to me from a source beyond myself. Slowly, my simplistic views of God and sentimental images of Jesus grew into a more mature understanding of the complexities of our human predicament. Reflecting on the early ages of my life, I am reminded of many incidents that capture my slow awareness, understanding, and transformation of what it means to respect the dignity of the other. My mind was captivated by the political and theological ideology justifying "separate development," which was later named *apartheid*, with its far-reaching prejudice and behavioral discriminations. Confirmation bias made the wrong things feel right. I was looking for evidence that supported me and our mistaken beliefs. It created a strong dissonance in my mind: what seemed right felt wrong. Peer pressure from the social circles I engaged in accepted many questionable behaviors, to which I felt I had to conform, even though I doubted their morality.

In my early twenties I experienced the real meaning of my name: King. Later, this meaning was expressed powerfully to me through the sixteenth-century painting of the calling of Matthew by Caravaggio. The characters in the painting are dressed in the typical aristocratic fashion of their day.

It was only when I vicariously entered this silent painting, that I began to understand *vocation*: In a public place, sitting at a table, are three tax collectors, with Matthew at the center. To the right of the table is Jesus, standing, with an outstretched left hand, pointing to Matthew—a gesture that implies,

"Matthew!"

Matthew, with a surprised expression, points to himself, which communicates,

"Who, me?"

"Yes, you! Follow me!"

And then, as I gazed into the Caravaggio ...

"Rex!"

"Who, me?"

"Yes, you! I have called you by your name. You belong to me. You are a son of the King and my friend!"

"But Lord, I often feel more like a prince in pauper's clothes—scruffy and dirty!"

As I matured in my journey towards wholeness, I understood the deeper meaning and consequences of Jesus saying and claiming, "I am [the Christ]" (John 8:58). Thus, I am baptized to be *Rex*!

Considering, knowing, and living my identity authentically, I have often reflected on the significance of prayers, specifically my prayers. I often prayed:

> Lord, throughout my life I have made my supplications known to you.
>
> You have never responded to my pleadings in a dramatic fashion or with miracles.
>
> You have only responded in silence—no audible word, nothing.
>
> Yet, I have noticed your reply.
>
> You responded softly and delicately.
>
> You made me notice and hear your Spirit, like a soft rustle of the leaves in a still evening breeze.

In these movements of solitude, I often heard leaves fall to the ground—a sign of a season of death and decay, waiting for a new season to transform into new life. I have become aware of and appreciate the presence of these *petites miracles*—little miracles—how God moves in our lives in many and often unexpected ways. The sun rises and sets each day; small seeds grow into mighty trees; a bird sings; a flower blooms; the many components of our body work together, enabling us to breathe, run, dream, and eat. Then there are the many synchronicities—an unexpected phone call from a friend to which I respond, "What a surprise! I thought of you this morning," or unexpectedly finding a word or a verse that speaks to a present concern. I have cultivated a sense of awe and wonder in everyday events that I am often too busy, too distracted, or too disillusioned, to see and recognize as *little miracles*. Yet, I recognize a spiritual need that calls me to cultivate a better sense of awe and wonder in the world. This is what recognizing everyday miracles means—that God not only intervenes on rare occasions but is always present in a variety of human experiences.

In this reflection, I rely primarily on events, interactions, and relationships in my own story. This, my participative knowing, requires an attempt at understanding how I grasped and was shaped by experience, in a remembered sense of presence, and that my awareness of a situation is located fully in my own perspective as a white, Christian, Afrikaner, privileged man. My written account may not ring true for every reader and should be corroborated or even corrected and expanded by other descriptions. Jacques Ellul reminds me that "being written down has not changed [the truth] or its aim, meaning, or intention. It is just diluted, weaker, and no longer backed up by a person's whole being."[2]

I have no reluctance to recognize the significance of integration in my or anyone's life. The truth is that it is not I who initiated or effected the integration in my life. Therefore, it is not unimportant that I grew up in a middle-class Afrikaner family and community, a member of the Reformed Church; that I married and had my own family of four children; that my career as a clinical psychologist and psychotherapist at the University of Pretoria ended when I became Dean at Saint Augustine College of South Africa; and that I am a member of an Anglican congregation in Irene, in Gauteng. Writing my thoughts is like a weaver's loom lifting thousands of threads as memory shuttles back and forth, struggling through recollections, words, and phrases to truly express myself.

EARLY ACADEMIC PATHWAYS

Politically, as a white Afrikaner male who had benefitted from the system of apartheid personally and academically, I was an infant. Never an activist or a conscientious objector, I was always striking camp in the Afrikaner laager. The Afrikaner student community was passive, never actively protesting like the National Union of South African Students (NUSAS) or the South African Students' Organisation (SASO). My political awakening and enlightenment began at the age of eighteen during a scholarship year in the United States in 1964. Before that year I was indoctrinated with quick answers to justify apartheid. In the US and thereafter, in personal encounters with African students, it dawned on me

2. Ellul, *Humiliation of the Word*, 44–45.

that something was seriously wrong in South Africa's social and political order. *Why did whites hold on to power so brutally?* How demeaning our public life was, with "Whites Only" signs in all restaurants and public amenities.

During the 1960s, the tension between South Africa's isolation and international globalization became noticeable. On the one hand, South Africa was characterized by an increasingly rigid, static system of governance and a totalitarian political philosophy, while on the other, the country entered the global imagination as Dr. Christiaan Barnard performed the world's first heart transplant in Cape Town on December 3, 1967. Less than two years later, on a more global scale, another "transplant" took place, on July 16, 1969, when Apollo 11 launched to the moon, landing on July 20. A first-time feat for human feet. These years were also the era of a truly mass popular culture, exemplified in the global celebrity status of the Beatles and culminating in the release of their recording masterpiece in 1967—*Sgt. Pepper's Lonely Hearts Club Band.*

During this defining decade, a transplant of various psychological, philosophical, and theological ideas took place. The 1960s represented the threshold between modernity and postmodernity. Yet in South Africa, white South Africans were living on something of an information island. State press censorship was enforced, and the introduction of television was still some way off. Very little was known about the devastation of the war in Vietnam and the growing disenchantment of US citizens with their country's involvement. White South African students hardly understood the origin, reason, and consequences of the 1968 Paris student uprising. From the "winds of change" speech by British Prime Minister, Harold MacMillan, to the South African parliament, these winds blew everywhere, but not in South Africa. It was a time of economic boom coupled with a subdued political climate—an uneasy calm before the storm of the 1970s. As a result of South Africa's apartheid policy in sports, on May 15, 1970, the International Olympic Movement expelled the country from the International Olympic Committee. In the same year, the English Cricket Council bowed to British government pressure and called off the all-white South African cricket tour. Thus began a cultural boycott in the 1970s, which peaked with the murder of Steve Biko in 1977 and continued until the early 1990s.

From 1972 onwards, the cultural boycott took shape in full force and had a devastating impact on my academic career. For example, cultural exchange between South African and Dutch scholars was officially terminated. No academic books were allowed to be imported for tertiary education purposes. Up to this point the Dutch language provided, at least for Afrikaans-speaking scholars, access to Continental thinking. The cultural boycott certainly contributed, even if only indirectly, to the demise of the apartheid political system. For thirty years, Afrikaans secondary school children and university students would remain so much the poorer because of the loss of this window to the arts, culture, and scholarship in Europe.

On the other hand, American publishing companies always found ways to circumvent the boycott. The result was that the thinking of generations of students between the 1970s and 1990s was significantly formed through American textbooks. During these years, 90 percent of prescribed tertiary textbooks were authored by American scholars.

Apartheid politics unsurprisingly bedeviled South Africans' participation in international events. I experienced this firsthand in 1986 when I applied to participate in a seminar in Perugia, Italy. My proposed paper was accepted on condition that I formulate my position in respect of apartheid. After much consideration, I formulated a personal statement on my ethical and moral rejection of apartheid, expressing my understanding of the damage the system of apartheid had done to the human dignity and freedom of most of the people in South Africa. On my arrival, the first order of business was a discussion of my statement and my participation in the seminar. There was a strong opposition to my participation, particularly from the Scandinavian and Dutch scholars. After lengthy deliberation, the meeting decided I could participate on condition that the meeting write a formal letter of protest to the

South African government, which had to include my original statement.

A few weeks after my return to South Africa, I was summoned to the office of the Vice-Chancellor of the University of Pretoria and asked to explain the meaning of a letter received from the Department of Foreign Affairs. I was severely reprimanded for placing the university in a position of criticism against the government.

Several psychology scholars wrote convincingly, providing a solid profile of the silence on racism in our discipline and the lack of resistance to apartheid. However, there are counterexamples that showcased the inhumanity of apartheid and the desecration of human dignity by apartheid laws. For several years after the mid-1970s, I was given the task of teaching a semester course in social psychology, on prejudice in ethics. Teaching about race stereotypes, prejudice, and discrimination during the height of apartheid, was a small contribution to address and create awareness about the pathology of racism and its destructive consequences for South Africans.

The silence on racism extended into various areas of society, including many denominations and churches. Bill Houston, whom I knew as National Director of the Students' Christian Association (SCA), gives a good account of this time when he writes,

> One of the distressing facts of those days was that the evangelical and Pentecostal churches by and large gave no lead nor critical biblical reflection on apartheid. The mantra of the time was that "Christianity and politics should not mix." Political activism was largely confined to the ecumenical wing of the church, especially among Roman Catholics, and to some brave Dutch Reformed leaders. One noteworthy exception was the SCA Student Declaration of 1980. This declaration was subsequently published in the Journal of Theology for Southern Africa.[3]

3. Houston, "Student's Christian Association," 16.

My involvement and participation in SCA discipleship courses had a profound influence on every aspect of my life. The new relationships and insights SCA provided, widened me to become a more mature Christian. I became drawn to Afrikaner dissident thinkers because of my involvement with SCA, yet I was without what might today be referred to as "struggle credentials."

It remains inexplicable that South Africa was so out of pace with world opinion regarding dignity and human rights. Most National Party Afrikaners were not open to anything that acknowledged the equality of black people or the dignity of the individual. Apartheid's effective social engineering of the relationship between white and black South Africans was the status quo. It was hard to understand the prejudice and discrimination underpinning white, especially Afrikaner, politics. Apparently, God was on our side, and we were the chosen people, endangered after World War II, in a new Cold War, by what Afrikaner theologians and politicians often referred to colloquially as *die rooi gevaar, die swart gevaar, en die Roomse gevaar.*[4]

IN SEARCH OF SOUL AND STATE AND CHRIST

The fall of the Berlin Wall in 1989 was the inspiration for Leonard Cohen's song "Democracy," which he did not complete until three years later. Hearing this song for the first time in the mid-1990s moved me. It is an intimate and affirming song about the experiment of democracy in the US. Post-apartheid South Africa is rather similarly already an experiment, a laboratory of constitutional democracy, where people of different classes, genders, and sexual orientations, encounter one another. In my reverie, I adapted the lyrics of Leonard Cohen's "Democracy" to the South African context, replacing "USA" with "RSA" in the lyrics so that I could hear and sing about democracy in South Africa.

4. "The red peril, the black peril, and the Roman peril."

Although I was joyful and hopeful at the arrival of a "new South Africa," I knew that when the dam wall of apartheid broke, the flooding of fresh water over dry land and people would also bring much debris, which for me symbolizes a dialectic between state of soul—my soul and the soul of the state, the South African state—an idea I borrow from Theodore Roszak: the fate of the soul is the fate of the social order.[5]

As a psychology student I explored the terms *soul*, *psyche*, and *mind* in some depth. Unlike traditional definitions that often link the soul to religious or spiritual contexts, the meaning of "soul" in a more nuanced, psychological sense, with a more distinctive and expansive meaning, can be understood as the human connection to imagination, dreams, and myth. The soul is the source of our deepest emotions, thoughts, and creativity, operating through symbols and images rather than rational thought.

I began to sense that my soul (my personhood) embodied depth and multiplicity, a realm where opposites and paradoxes, ambiguity, and complexity coexist. I began to learn to engage with my inner life and the symbolic dimensions of experience, viewing the soul as a dynamic and integral part of both individual and collective existence—the state of my soul and the soul of the state.

In my early twenties I read psychology, philosophy, and theology, discovering that in all three monotheistic religions, God *speaks* and God's *word* is pivotal. In the Afrikaner worldview of that time, the word of God was supposed to have formed the history of Afrikaner culture and western civilization. I was wondering, *Who is God? Does the word "God" have any meaning for us today?* In a world after Auschwitz, I felt we could no longer believe in the omnipotence of God. An omnipotent God is useless and cannot affirm the meaning of human existence. *How could I understand and account for the fact that I knew many men and women who found it liberating to be rid of God, this vengeful deity whose rules they had abided?* For some, the idea of God negated our freedom. So, then my thought was, *What is Christian freedom?* The key teachings of Christian faith were being contemptuously discarded.

5. Roszak, *Where the Wasteland Ends*, 144.

And what was left? All talk about God became confusing and staggered under impossible contradictions.

My existential bafflement became more intense. Human relationships and the quest for self-realization became more complex and puzzling to me, which raised difficult questions about self and individuation. The more I understood the depth, height, and width of human experience, the more baffled my fellow human beings and I appeared to be.

As my journey continued, I came to understand that God's ideal and love for humanity might indeed lead me to become more fully human. I was "given" encounters with men and women who provided both comfort and challenge, as I wrestled with bafflement about my and our existence.

I went beyond questions about the historical Jesus, which for me is a historical futility, and rather became awed and fascinated by Jesus as the archetypal stranger, from nowhere, shrouded in mystery. The great "I am," who said "It is I; don't be afraid!" (John 6:20). A Jesus who is not interested in legalistic ethics, but a Jesus who is concerned with me, paralyzed in my human condition—concerned with *righting my being*, restoring my character out of balance, crossing out what I am not, and empowering me by his Spirit.

During my training as a psychotherapist, one of my mentors blindfolded me while he was role-playing a patient. This forced me to listen more carefully rather than to look and observe. From that valuable experience, I created a personal mantra: "In an interpersonal, conversational context, one cannot see the truth but only hear the truth."

Through apartheid, a distorted view of reality was created. Events and information had to fit the ideology of the state to perpetuate economic inequality and injustice. Those who opposed or challenged this dominant ideology would face persecution, imprisonment, or worse. I read a second-hand paperback copy of Plato's *Republic* at the age of eighteen. I did not understand much of what I read. Only years later, did I realize that Plato provides a root metaphor for a dialectic between the paranoid state of a soul and the soul of a state. In Plato's eyes, this relationship is characterized by "pervasive and unwarranted suspiciousness and mistrust," and is a relationship that "questions the loyalty" of those who are "unwilling to submit." Plato's state has an "inordinate fear of losing power to shape events in accordance with [its] own wishes." The greatest mark of the soul-state relationship for Plato is "mistrust between the governed and their government."[6] I was now asking, *Is it possible to de-ideologize reality? How do we unfix theology from its revelational delusion, and politics from the paranoid soul of the state?*

Even now, thirty years into a new dispensation of constitutional democracy, the grip of ideology and signs of the paranoid soul of the state remain visible: the state confuses welfare with security, and the common good with political strength.

Religions may present a vision of a just society but do not easily have practical political programs in the form of laws and policies. The emphasis of religion is on faith and worship; its appeal is to inwardness and its aim, the redemption or purification and wholeness of the human spirit. An ideology speaks to the group, the nation, or the class. The ideas, however, show little concern with epistemology, or how we know what we know. Rather, ideology, even religious ideology, is primarily concerned with human progress, particularly by political means. Politics, in its broadest sense, imposes itself on everything. I never questioned if Christians should participate in politics. We do so out of necessity. Bonhoeffer, Hauerwas, Bosch, and Yoder, show convincingly that Christianity is a politics, an alternative politics to the status quo—the politics of Jesus and the politics of the kingdom, which is a politics that is necessarily subversive of empire.

My question is to know how to participate in society in such a way as to bring a certain freedom into this order, to manifest Christian freedom within it. There is no "Christian reason" why I should be more to the right than to the left, or vice versa. The left's conviction is about progress for the disadvantaged, as well as their belief that there are unjustified inequalities that need to be reduced

6. Hillman, *On Paranoia*, 49.

or abolished through radical means. To change the nature of the society is no more Christian than the rightist ideas of country, hierarchy, national culture, identity, economy, honor, and order. Equally respectable values are found on both sides. To formulate theological arguments in justification for a chosen position, as the Reformed churches did in South Africa, seems wrong.

So, what then? What is Christian freedom?

For me, the key ideas are the kingdom of God as a root metaphor for which there is no definition, least of all being defined by democracy. Jesus is a "parable of God," the Alpha and Omega, the source of all revealed truth, and God's glory is our goal, in which everything in life finds its answer. He called me by my name. *Can I truly confess that he is everything from A to Z in my life? Is every phase of my life inspired by his Spirit?*

OUR STORIES TO LIVE BY IN LATER LIFE

Recently, I retired. By the grace of God, I have few aches and pains for my age. From a certain point of view, I am a statistic: in 2012, there were 810 million people in the world of sixty years and older, almost 12 percent of the total world population. By 2015, this number would double. Around the world, two people turn sixty years old every second. My life expectancy is eighty years and more. For every one hundred females of eighty years and older, there are only eighty-four males. I know that like most retirees, I am concerned about the security of my income so that I can meet my obligations. Although I am relatively healthy, I wonder if I will still have access to age-friendly and affordable medical care. I also wonder if I will live in an environment that would support my growing old when I become less mobile and weaker in my senses and memory. I know that the local community I now live in is not homogeneous. Our retirees are just as diverse as any other age group. I still want to stay active and be a respected member of society. Like most other retirees, I want to be productive and contribute in some way.

Yet, I am much more than just a statistic. I do not want to be reduced to some social and demographic category. I know that my progress into old age has physical, cultural, psychological, and spiritual challenges. The bigger picture helps me understand and accept that growing old is inevitable. Although retirement does not typically lead to existential crises, it did confront me with an existential challenge. The children were taken care of, each self-reliant on their own life path. As children leave their parents' home, many parents experience a painful goodbye, followed by the "empty nest." In my case, there was an "empty nest dream." With expectation, I met my retirement as one of the thresholds in a new trimester of my life. My retirement was not indicative of a fixed, unchanging, static state, but more of a dynamic attitude towards life in which personal unfolding and development occurs. I would venture on in faith come what may.

Over time, I discovered that the psychic and spiritual demands and pitfalls, such as pride and selfishness, also tempted me. Over the centuries, previous generations have defied them, using symbols, spiritual practice, and other sources of wisdom. The religious tradition in which we stand does not always contain wisdom for questions of life that each of us face on our own. When we seek wisdom, the guidance available is not always formative. The problem is that the natural science worldview of our time is so dominant that all "gods and devils" have been removed from our inner landscape and rationalized away. Our inner life has become inaccessible and invisible, as if in a solar eclipse. For us as postmodern humans, the cosmos is no longer mesmerizing as it was in classical times. It sometimes leaves us alone, confused, and doubtful. In this virtual-reality–shaped world, we must find and create the meaning of our lives, ourselves. It is an arduous odyssey in these logical and yet fragmented times. Still, in our wealth of stories, myths, and legends, there are important clues about the course of each person's personal, inner, social, political, and outer journey. This is the challenge: how to locate the rules and make sense of the game before the Referee blows the final whistle.

In my familial, social, personal, and professional roles, like most other people, I have been through countless chrysalises, losses, and disappointments. Also through many tests, successes, temptations, betrayals, ecstasies, and numerous unique encounters with all kinds of people. On several critical thresholds of each decade of my adult life, I was forced to reflect, sometimes deliberately, on my own story. Secretly, I thought that a lot of good things were still to come, and that at my age I had a little wisdom and was well prepared for what lay ahead—like a warrior and hero, my mindset was one of excited anticipation and readiness, come what may.

The Old Testament narrative of Israel's forty-year wandering in the desert to the promised land, and the classical myth of Odysseus, the leader and hero of Homer's *Odyssey*, share many points of contact with the pattern of my life. Here I want to weave my discovery of the significance, for my retirement and for the mature and latter stages of my life, of what Homer wrote in 700 BC.[7]

Odysseus returned to his island after fifty years of wanderings and adventures to reunite with his beloved wife, Penelope, his old father, Laertes, his longing son, Telemachus, and even his dying old dog, Argos. After he made landfall no one recognized him except an old housemaid. He pleaded with her not to tell anyone, at least for now, that he had returned.

(It may sometimes also be the case that women do not "recognize" their husbands after their long careers—so many hours absent from home. A woman may find it difficult to find her way when "her man returns." She may experience him as "under her feet." It might then take time and tolerance to "find one another" once again.)

Unlike Odysseus, nothing could prepare me for what was to come in my odyssey. I was on my way back after the voyage, to "my island," but while still "at sea" a tsunami rose up and overwhelmed me. My children and I lost my wife, their mother, in a sudden, incomprehensible tragedy. My ideal destination, my "island," vanished. One half disappeared under the water. In mourning, dazed and lost, I remained on the remaining wasteland for months. All my dreams for the period before my retirement and after were

7. My source was the authoritative translation of Homer in English. So, John William Mackail.

swallowed by the dark water. After months I returned to the sea, directionless and without a compass.

Odysseus returned and reunited with his wife, his son, and his father. With stories like these we expect heroes to "live happily ever after." However, what on the surface would seem like an appropriate ending, was not to be. Homer wrote two final chapters, a kind of epilogue. He announced that Odysseus was going on a new and second journey. Instead of quietly retiring, he was reminded of a prophecy he received long before, from the blind seer, Tiresias. Thus, he had to leave his home again. This was his fate, and the gods expected it of him. His second journey is not described in detail but written down in a few striking paragraphs. Perhaps this serves as a literary antecedent of what may happen to many of us. Here is my summary of the key elements:

First, Odysseus had received this prophecy during one of the low points of his wanderings, as he traveled through the "kingdom of the dead." It is true that sometimes we hear better when we experience a low point, our ego broken and weakened.

Second, Tiresias appeared like a ghost, with a golden scepter in his hand, and gave Odysseus the message. The golden scepter is perhaps a symbol of an authoritative message from the heavens.

Third, Tiresias told Odysseus, "You must make a good quality oar and carry it far, not on your island, but deep into the mainland interior. You carry it until you arrive in a country with people who have never been to the sea, who do not even mix salt into their food. They know nothing about ships and oars."[8] Odysseus had to leave the comfort of his home—his island—and enter the hinterland, the "interior": the island versus the hinterland; the part versus the whole; the outer world versus a world more inward; the small picture and the wider vista. To connect these parts and unite them into a whole is a religious, spiritual experience. The journey into the interior connects us to our inner world. It is a task of the

8. My paraphrases of Homer's plot in the *Odyssey* indicated with quotation marks here and in what follows rehearse events in Mackail's "Epilogue of the Odyssey," bk. 23 (Mackail, *Odyssey*, 304–24), with close reference to bk. 11 (79–89, 136–37).

later part of our lives, after the first forty years, before, during, and after retirement.

Also, he had to carry the oar. For me, this signifies all the "tools" I have gathered and used in the first half of my life. Homer writes that the inland resident told him, "[I see that] you are carrying a pitchfork on your shoulder." He saw the oar as a pitchfork, with which chaff is separated from wheat. Odysseus had to plant the oar right then and there, firmly in the ground, and leave it there. Only then could he return home. I planted my oar "right then and there"—the tools with which I had worked so productively—and then I "just left." For me, this experience was a whole new separation of chaff from wheat.

After that, Odysseus sacrificed three animals: a storm ram, a breeding pig, and a breeding bull—striking images of masculinity, male vitality, strength, and instinctive reactions. Also symbolic of the power of reproductive energy, fertility, and stubbornness that sometimes borders on blind assertiveness and unchecked emotion.

SEPARATING THE WHEAT FROM THE CHAFF

Continuing my journey and exploring the interior required me to give up something, to let something go—especially the sword and shield of the warrior and hero. I had to use other instruments of my human equipment. These mythic sacrifices also signify recognition of the Creator of the cosmos, and our place in and commitment to the kingdom of God.

Lastly, only after completing this further journey with its sacrifices would I live peaceably in myself and with people around me. Tiresias ends his prophecy with the words, "Your death will come from the sea. Your life will gently flow away like a low tide until your years are filled with peace in your heart."[9] Odysseus's second journey into the "interior" encouraged me greatly. The

9. My paraphrase of the prophecy of Tiresias to Odysseus in book 11 of Homer's *Odyssey*. Butler, *Odyssey*, 137–43.

question that comes to my mind after all is, *How do I separate the wheat from the chaff?*

God created me with the ability to love and the option to reject that love; the ability to trust, and the freedom to doubt; the ability to make choices, and, also, the responsibility to face and accept the consequences. The crux of this peculiar difficulty lies in the fact that many times I refuse to acknowledge how carnal I am. Like something foul smelling that is hidden by perfume, or something cracked that is covered with white plaster. My imagined reinterpretations make me scoop out the gnats as if they were someone else's fault and then swallow a camel. My mind remains closed, veiled. My prayer becomes a plea: "Lord take away the veil. Remove the veil over my face! Open my eyes!" If the veil is removed, I am "transformed into his [Christ's] image with ever-increasing glory" (2 Cor 3:18).

So many have said this in different ways; we all suffer a tragic case of incomplete or distorted identity. Life's journey calls for me to become myself with greater fullness, to become who I am meant to be. Veiled, I live from my social persona, sometimes also from a false self. Unveiled, I live from my true self.

If my life were not a search for the abundance I need, at once physically, interpersonally, morally, aesthetically, intellectually, and spiritually, then I would not be able to anchor myself firmly in the essential. I am aware of the balance between abundance and scarcity at all levels of my existence. I have planted my oar and have made my sacrifice of the bull, the pig, and the ram. From this I have learned that with an open heart and mind, and with a new discipline, I can trust my needs, and the discomfort I experience when my needs are not met, when compliance is almost unmanageable, as a good guide for my life. At my age, on my second journey, on my pathway to wholeness, this has led to outcomes that are far beyond my ability to tell.

In his invitation that encouraged us to contribute to this book, James Goddard concluded his introductory paragraph by stating,

> The following of Christ has been significantly shaped by social injustices, grief, and Christ's invitation to take courage and persevere in walking new pathways into wholeness.

The phrase "walking new pathways into wholeness" has richly occupied my reflections. I now share some diverse ideas as my contribution towards reaching some clarity on the meaning of wholeness and how being whole is realized.

The concept of wholeness is multifaceted, understood and utilized across various disciplines, including theology, philosophy, psychology, and even the natural sciences such as medicine and systems theory. Each perspective provides a unique interpretation of what it means to be whole, often reflecting the integration and harmonization of parts into a complete and cohesive framework.

Wholeness in spiritual and religious contexts often pertains to the integration of the individual with the Divine and the kingdom of God. Philosophy often examines wholeness in relation to metaphysics, ethics, and epistemology. In medicine and health, wholeness often refers to a holistic approach—to well-being. In psychology, wholeness often relates to the integration of the self and achieving mental health. Concepts such as individuation and self-actualization describe the process by which individuals integrate various parts of the psyche, conscious and unconscious, to achieve a sense of wholeness and self-realization, in which they realize their fullest potential, integrating aspects of their personality to achieve a whole, authentic self.

Wholeness is a concept that transcends disciplines, reflecting a universal desire for integration, balance, and unity. Whether viewed through the lens of theology, philosophy, or psychology, wholeness represents the harmonization of diverse elements into a coherent whole. Understanding these varied interpretations enriches our appreciation of the complexity and depth of wholeness.

Can I know that I am on a pathway towards wholeness? How might I know? Or would I only know through my relationships and experiences with others and God? How can I know with any degree of certainty the wholeness of myself or anyone else, living or dead?

Even more, can wholeness foster the integrity of identity and the cohesion of community? Does wholeness involve creating inclusive and supportive communities where diverse members can find harmony and cohesion while respecting individual differences?

The healing function of a community is to integrate the self by upholding us and enabling us to experience faith, hope, and love. Thus, wholeness of personhood is the responsibility of the community and not merely the responsibility of the self.

Parents, especially fathers, are representatives of right and justice. Even a small child already distinguishes very precisely between those commands that come from caprice, mood, and malice, and those that issue *for justice's sake*. Children are very sensitive to injustices, even when there is enough reasonable might behind unjust orders to carry them out. I hold the view that we are born with the potential for wholeness. *What then is "normal" and "healthy" humanity?* In debates between theologians and psychologists, this issue is often framed in terms of "wholeness and holiness." *Does normal, healthy personhood result from or depend upon an innate "holistic" self, or must one be "sanctified" by the Spirit of God to become whole? Is wholeness both a spiritual and psychological goal?* Given these questions, and the variety of interpretations that generate them, my contribution and elaboration here will not be too wide ranging.

During my teaching career, I often had to teach a senior course in personality psychology. I usually began by posing my foundational question, *Do you know and understand that you have personality and that you are a person?* I attempted to find a balance between lecturing on personality and personhood. I focused on the variety of descriptors of personality in the normative sense, as well as on two essential elements of recognizing a person: a face coupled with a name. Knowing and loving another human being involves a dialectical participation with the other. One must, broadly speaking, have at least a readiness to love the other, if one is to understand the other.

ATTACHMENT, DETACHMENT, AND LOSS IN THE SEVENTH AGE

In his famous verses on the seven stages of life,[10] Shakespeare reminds me that, at my age, I have passed through each of the life stages before I leave the stage of life itself.

In the later adult, mature stages of my life, at appropriate moments, I reflected prayerfully and with humility, on my existence. I thought about the balance of my life, a kind of in-between balance during the different stages, on my pathway towards an integrated, more completed life.

At different points in the ages of my life, and for different reasons, I attached and detached from something and someone. On the pathway to wholeness, it was necessary to separate in order to become. Separation served my growth, my becoming. I realized that separation as detachment is a form of "psychic surgery," a kind of amputation. A gap or wound appears, as happens in the loss of bereavement. With the death of loved ones, I was pulled between desires for attachment and separateness. I wanted the impossible: to lose my isolation and keep it at the same time. Attachments serve to create a foundation, joints or hinges, a place for living, while detachments create hollows or an opening—space for regenerating and renewing our future life.

The plurality of emotions I felt in my grieving made it difficult to pinpoint exactly what I was grieving about. We have all suffered the death and loss of colleagues, friends, family members, relationally further or close to us. To make sense of my grieving, I now reflect on three deaths of significant others at different points in my life:

First, Ockert, my best friend at university, at the age of twenty-one. One evening, as we crossed a road, a drunken driver crashed into us. Ockert died instantly, and I came away with some bruises.

Second, my father, known as Uncle Van, died in hospital at the age of eighty-two. I remember his last words, and I then softly

10. Shakespeare, "All the World's."

prayed next to his face, "Dad, through God's grace, he will honor your kindness and generosity."

And then, my dear wife, Marijke. She died inexplicably in ICU, after a standard neurosurgical back operation. The surgeon missed a surgical mistake. The medical team noticed it too late. With her death, my dream of enjoying my retirement with her was crushed. My sense of desolation is well expressed by the Czech artist Mucha's *Woman in the Wilderness* (1923). Grieving, I shouted, *Lord, are you forsaking me?* There was no answer—no explanation.

In all three instances I was bewildered and perplexed. I had lost dear ones and my relationship with them. The medical forensic postmortem reports may all have been written in medical scientific terms, but in each case, the object of my grief was my loss of loved ones, and my loss of the relationship with them. What matters to me about the ongoing relationships with these loved ones remains a work in progress. Often it seems to resolve itself, only to resurface unexpectedly. I often look back to the past relationships that I have lost. Often, with questions and conflicting feelings about who, and how, and when, and whether, I appreciated and loved their presence in my life—why their deaths matter so much to me, and who they were for me.

In the ongoing questions, I also looked ahead, to how my life would continue in the absence of ones whom I had so loved. There were moments when I thought, *How am I going to go on?* Marijke's death especially was, as someone noted, a "narrative disruption" in my life. The role that she played in my life, and my expectations of everyday living in the ongoing relationship with her, was irreparably altered through my bereavement. My sense of wholeness in the social world and my geographic locale—even my embodied existence—was shattered, and the open wounds led to moments of despair.

Yet, I have noticed a movement from ignorance about myself to a deeper self-knowledge, a reconstruction of what I knew about myself (including the support and guidance of a female Christian Jungian psychotherapist). This is a form of self-interrogation, an opportunity to relate to myself more fully and lovingly.

In conclusion, my relationship with Marijke continues, which reminds me of Pauline Boss's phrase, "Loss is ambiguous and has no resolution."[11] This thought challenged the generally acceptable idea that one should "find resolution" in the face of loss. This idea is different from "holding on" and "letting go." Yet, grief is probably the most taxing of life events. It is different from the loss of children leaving home, or a divorce. The loss of a significant other is "irreversible and irreplaceable."[12]

SOME CLOSING THOUGHTS

Everyday life experiences of South Africans during apartheid and thirty-two years into the new democracy remain horrifying for many citizens. We know that personhood is distorted by economic and class position and that the creation of social bonds is vital to societal and personal health and well-being. For all our brokenness, woundedness, fragmentation and alienation, our fundamental condition is one of belonging. This requires trust in the security of attachments, and, on the other hand, trust in the power of detachment, of leaving behind, of finding balance, and of the hope of transcendence.

Throughout the different ages of my life, and now specifically as a widower, I had to determine what was essential, and avoid what was inessential, by getting rid of many accumulated belongings, including many of my books. Aside from material objects, certain ideas also required me to discard or refine. The question of balance on my pathway is beautifully expressed by the Dutch artist Vermeer's 1664 painting *Woman Holding a Balance*. This work has been interpreted either as a message of temperance and moderation or as a representation of divine truth and justice.[13]

Delicately she holds a balance in her hand, while there are pieces of gold and pearls in front of her. Behind her is a painting

11. Boss, *Myth of Closure*, 190.

12. Boss, *Myth of Closure*, 17.

13. Vivanco, "Johannes Vermeer's Influence."

of the last judgment. This Vermeer painting can be interpreted in many ways. From a symbolic point of view, I ask, *What is being weighed?* Gold and pearls are indeed earthly goods of great value. *Or is her valued object something invisible, inner treasure that can never be grasped?* She is an example I need to follow. Like her, I must hold a balance in my hand, to measure, not from a moralistic perspective, but, like the painting of the last judgment on the wall behind her, as a counterweight might suggest, as a measure of the transcendent. Success, results, and recognition, can never be spiritual goals. What is weighed on the scale must be brought to a balance. The painting encouraged me to lead a balanced and thoughtful life. *What have I done thus far? Is there a balance between the vices and virtues in my life? Is my life in balance without external motivation, for example, my good health and my welfare or self-justification*?

Through faith I am exonerated, set free from my sinfulness. *Do you see this like I see it?* The temptations and accusations of self and others, or the doubtful honor of my experiences, have not burdened, enslaved, or damaged me, but, being exonerated, acquitted, completely cleared from accusation or charge and from any suspicion of blame or guilt, I am set free. This continued struggle with freedom on my journey to wholeness has led me to the ability to be enchanted in awe by Christ, who reveals to us a whole world and life, as life can really be lived.

Is wholeness the highest form of our humanity? Who can, without pretension, lay claim on perfection? Ultimately, my life has arrived at what is essentially unknowable. What I have experienced can never be defined or capture a finality in formulas. Reality is unfathomable and inexhaustible, always challenging and breaking loose from many of my concepts. Whatever path I walk, whether from the inside out or from the outside in, the goal is the same: to realize that in the final matters of life and death I am, we are, animated by a single light. The one Light is not just a metaphor but a loving power, a living energy. My life, in this living energy, is a life in Christ, who invites me to note: As he was crucified, Jesus completed the message of his life. He is the perfect one and he invites us towards this perfection, this pathway to wholeness, when he says in Matt 5:48, "Be perfect, therefore, as your heavenly Father is perfect."

CHAPTER FOUR

Compassion's Footprints Towards Wholeness

Faure Louw

In each of us, there are stories that await the right moment to come to light and reveal their power.

ADRIANA MÜLLER

SOME FIRST THOUGHTS

Life is a tapestry woven from the threads of narratives, each strand contributing to the rich fabric of our meaning-making and authoring of life experiences. We each weave our tapestry within our social context with the threads of our values, experiences, and relationships. We are born into and live in our stories and relationships, where we cocreate meaning through language. I realize that sharing my story is an act of interpretation, so I invite you, the reader, into my story—my experiences, relationships, and multivocal personal narratives—a contextual story of emotions, actions, relationships, embodiment, spirituality, reflections, values, pain, fears, joy, disillusionment, and hope. I write from my heart, not because I know, but to discover and author my being, relationships, culture, and social environment. I have learned that "Autoethnography is research, story writing, and method that connect the autobiographical and personal to the cultural, social and political."[1] For me this implies vulnerability—living consciously, emotionally, and reflexively. It asks that I consider how and why I think, act, and experience as I do. It is an intersubjective activity of storytelling, a reciprocal act that contributes to the personal, cultural, political, and social construction of my identity and meaning-making. The autoethnography and story-work of Travis Heath and others[2] challenges us to share the ethics, meaning, and spirit of our stories in ways that relieve, heal, and help make sense of our struggles in the present. I trust my story will testify to the grace and love of God, in whom "we live and move and have our being" (Acts 17:28).

I will write from a narrative therapy perspective and will therefore personify and externalize problems to create a distance between a person and a problem, to negotiate a relationship with life's problems. I will also personify Compassion and invite her and her colleagues as companions, to cocreate the meaning of my journey, through conversations and letters.

I was inspired to use letters by Denise Ackermann, who uses letter writing as a medium of vicarious communication with people significant to her.[3] Letters are personal, experiential, conversational, and relational. They can be revisited or even continued. They document life and author identity, to connect and interpret the themes of our lives. I will use letter writing to revisit my past experiences and reflect on how they contribute to the authoring of my life, my identity, and my journey with God during trying times. The stories I share are interrelated and are windows into my faith journey in the context of justice, grief, hope, and wholeness in Christ. I will follow the footprints of Compassion in my life, in

1. Ellingson and Ellis, "Autoethnography as Constructionist Project," 450.
2. Heath et al., *Reimagining Narrative Therapy.*
3. Ackermann, *After the Locusts.*

conversation with Compassion, who has journeyed with me since childhood through experiences of injustice and grief, towards wholeness and *shalom*.

DISCOVERING COMPASSION

Shortly after my birth my mother started writing letters to me, documenting stories of my birth, environment, experiences, and relationships. She wrote,

> When I was in the maternity hospital with you when you were born, there was a baby boy born prematurely. His mom didn't have breast milk for him. I was so happy that I had enough for you and him. After a week, when he was strong enough to go home, I thanked God that I could contribute to his life.

She also included this stamp in a letter.

The legend goes that Father Edward Flanagan, founder of the children's home Boys Town, saw a boy, Reuben Granger, carrying another boy up some stairs—Howard Loomis, who had had polio and wore leg braces. Flanagan asked Granger if carrying Loomis was difficult. The boy replied, "He isn't heavy, Father; he's my brother." This is a metaphor for my father's life of serving orphans and abandoned children, honoring and continuing a family tradition of four generations of involvement with orphanages. Nobody's circumstances and pain were too heavy for him to carry, often at personal cost.

Why did my mother choose to write up my story? Why did she specifically choose these two stories? What does it say about her and my father? What was her message to me? Also, how did these stories influence and coauthor my life, values, and way of being?

I grew up as eldest and only son with four sisters, in Zimbabwe, on the outskirts of Harare, where my father was the director of Bothashof, a church school and children's home. Children needing special care often lived in our home. As children we were aware of other children who did not have family and a home as we had. It was there that I experienced how my parents shared their lives. Regarding my mother's story, it was not so much the act of sharing her breast milk but sharing and sustaining a life *where nobody was too heavy to be carried.* For my parents, their way of being practiced a legacy of love, compassion, and care. *In their way of life and service, I encountered you, Compassion, witnessing and experiencing your presence!*

I recall an early childhood experience of injustice. Elias, originally from Damaraland in Namibia, and Afrikaans-speaking, was the driver of our school bus. One Sunday, he drove the children to church, and being black and aware of the racial practice of worshiping separately, he waited outside. My mother invited him to sit at the back of the church, but he was chased out by a church elder who maintained that this church was for whites only. "There is a separate church for blacks," he said. "He should attend there."

I witnessed Elias's indignation and my mother's embarrassment and anger. Back home, our parents revisited with us this experience of pain, injustice, and disrespect that my mother and Elias had experienced. Suddenly, I became aware of racial injustice, discrimination, and the polarization in our society.

This is the family into which I was born—a community of love, compassion, and care. I was given space to discover myself, author my own story and identity, and create a context, even before I had language to name or give meaning to my experiences. O'Hanlon says,

> Like clay thrown on a potter's wheel we are shaped from the moment of our birth, not only by our family legacy, but by the culture that creates the way we see and talk about ourselves in the world.[4]

To trace the footprints of Love, Compassion, and Care in my life, I will converse with some of the influential participants in my story. The first conversation is with Compassion, who also introduced me to her relatives: among others, Justice and Reconciliation.

Compassion, you have been present and active in my life from early childhood, but I did not know your name. You participated in my mother's discovery of motherhood, empowered her to share her breast milk with a baby not her own. You were well-known in my family home and tradition, respected and influential, and you contributed to our being a family, a community. As a child, this gave me much comfort and security. Your presence became more real and important to me as I grew up. I needed you, and you influenced and motivated me, yet I never "saw" you, and often wondered what your name was, and what you "looked like." But I witnessed how you practiced your presence in relationships I was part of, or invited into.

I was curious to know your age, and how our relationship began—only to discover that I had inherited you like DNA. You featured strongly in the previous five generations of my paternal family. I traced your footprints back to my great-great grandfather, Andrew Murray Sr. (1794–1866), the Scottish pioneer minister and evangelical leader. He was born into a pious Aberdeenshire family and studied at Aberdeen University, where he felt called to be a missionary. He later responded to a call to South Africa, arriving in Cape Town on July 1, 1822, never to return to his country of birth.

His ministry in Graaff-Reinet lasted forty-five years until his death in 1866. With you, Compassion, he played a significant role in the religious life of South Africa. He married Maria Stegman and

4. O'Hanlon, "Third Wave," 19.

had eleven children. Five of the sons became ministers of religion, and four of his daughters married ministers. One of the sons, Andrew Murray (Junior), was the well-known evangelist and author of many books. Another son, Charles, succeeded his father at Graaff-Reinet and served the congregation for a further thirty-eight years. One of the daughters of Andrew Murray (Senior), Jemima, married Andries Adriaan Louw, a minister in Paarl, and another of their sons, Abraham (Affie) Louw, my grandfather, was later called to join his uncle Charles as second minister in Graaff-Reinet.[5]

An example of how you, Compassion, were instrumental in the ministry of both Charles and Abraham was how you made them aware of the poverty and poor living conditions of so many Graaff-Reinet families. It is told that hungry, malnourished children often rang the doorbell of the parsonage, asking for a piece of bread. Abraham recalled that one Saturday, while he was preparing his Sunday sermon, a gentleman arrived from a neighboring town with five boys, left them in my grandfather's care, and returned home.

In 1895, the parliament of the Cape Colony in Cape Town passed a law that made provision for a magistrate to remove children from their homes if their parents were unable to care for them, and place them in places of safety. With the encouragement of a local member of parliament, Abraham, Charles, and his wife, under this new law, opened a first house of safety for seven boys. This house grew rapidly and at least fifteen other children's homes or orphanages were developed after this one, due to your clear call and lasting presence in our family over five generations.

My parents' stay in Zimbabwe included a time of political conflict between Britain and Rhodesia, which in the end led to a "Unilateral Declaration of Independence" (UDI) by the white Rhodesian government. This, in turn, polarized and caused racial tension between the local population and the white government, resulting in a thirteen-year "Bush War" between government and liberation movements.

Reflecting on this period in my life, I realize how I struggled with the relationship between you, Compassion, and Protest. I

5. Louw, *My Eerste Neëntig Jaar.*

discovered that Protest was indeed one of your closest companions. My question was, "How should I position myself against injustices in society in my context of UDI and war?" I have since learned that Christ's compassion entails acceptance, forgiveness, and reconciliation, and this should inform my manner of protest.

As a Grade Eleven scholar, I walked naïvely into uncharted landscapes in my young Christian faith. My uncle was a missionary in Nyasaland (Malawi) and invited me to attend a Student Christian Movement (SCM) conference, where I was introduced to the East Africa Revival movement. This significant Christian renewal movement began in the late 1920s and 1930s. It originated in what was then the Belgian Ruanda-Urundi, and during the 1930s and 1940s, spread to various regions, including the eastern mountains of Belgian Congo, Uganda, Tanganyika, and Kenya. The revival emphasized a personal relationship with Christ, faith, high ethical and moral standards, strong bonds of fellowship, reconciliation across all boundaries, and a strong emphasis on 1 John 1:5–7:

> *This is the message we have heard from him and declare to you: God is light; in him there is no darkness at all. If we claim to have fellowship with him yet walk in the darkness, we lie and do not live out the truth. But if we walk in the light, as he is in the light, we have fellowship with one another, and the blood of Jesus, his Son, purifies us from all sin.*

This newfound fellowship superseded existing boundaries of tribe, color, class, and gender, so that hostility broke down and gave way to love and respect.

I was touched and inspired by the compassion and testimonies of some previous Mau Mau freedom fighters, in their commitment to Christ; I was introduced to the power of reconciliation. I recall the testimony of one of the delegates. He had been a dedicated Mau Mau and hated white settler colonists. He carried a list with three names of settlers whom he had to murder in the name of freedom. Then he came into faith in Christ. "I then discovered what freedom and reconciliation was about."

The movement since the revival still influences the morals and ethics, spiritual language, and practices of Protestant churches and communities in East Africa today. Revival principles and practices have been woven into the fabric of East African Christian communities. This, your spirit, Compassion, with Reconciliation, was especially seen in Kenya during the Mau Mau uprising. During the time when the Europeans were the object of hate and violence, because of colonial policies, Christians of different races remained faithful to each other. A striking feature of the revival was the breaking down of racial distrust and separation.

By now, you, Compassion, had a name, and I had experienced and witnessed your presence and way of being in the lives of my family, my teachers, the revival movement, and the faith community. Compassion, you often reminded me that Jesus wept when he saw the crowds who worried and were helpless "like sheep without a shepherd" (Matt 9:36). And then you invited me to walk hand in hand with you and with Tears, to grieve with those in grief, and to weep with those who wept in their pilgrimage towards Wholeness and Hope. I thank you.

You also helped me early in my life to move beyond a modernist, dogmatic, structuralist, and prescriptive theology. I moved from a judgmental, powerful God who had to be feared, towards a loving God who cares, who is relational, vulnerable, and comes to live with humanity as One who is weak and suffers—a God who died for me in the contradictions, confrontations, and pain of this world.

Daniel Louw argues for a "theology of the intestines," to describe God's passionate presence to the reality of human suffering in injustice, poverty, violence, stigmatization, discrimination, and power abuse—God's bowels contract on our behalf.[6] *Such compassion gives meaning to life. Jesus' bowels contracted when he saw the crowd was without bread. God's nature is the self-emptying, other-oriented, and sacrificial love that is fully displayed in the crucifixion. The passion of Christ expresses God's habitation of human vulnerability and suffering. Compassion, this is where I experienced you demonstrating and performing God's love in a world of injustice.*

6. Louw, "On Facing," 6–7.

Looking back on the East African Revival, my final school years, my theological studies, and my marriage, during which I moved to South Africa, I realize that this was a period of spiritual discovery, excitement, and romanticism—a period of understanding God and the world with naïveté. In the new environment of South Africa, I was exposed to the ideology and theology of apartheid, and to racial conflict, polarization, enmity, protests, and violence. I was uncertain and challenged about how you, Compassion, would accompany me in these new, uncertain times. However, you introduced me to lecturers and influential leaders who had a long and committed relationship with you. These people who knew your heart were like prophets of God's love, justice, and reconciliation, and were dissenting voices against apartheid, sometimes under very challenging circumstances, but always loyal and respectful.

I recall four lecturers: Prof. Ben Marais, professor of church history; Prof. Andre du Toit, our student chaplain and later lecturer in New Testament studies; and Prof. Johan Heyns, professor of systematic theology, well-known for his opposition to apartheid and his efforts to promote racial reconciliation. They were dedicated lecturers, mentors, pastors, and fellow pilgrims on my journey towards wholeness. Ben Marais was also house master of Sonop, our student residence. He had a personal interest in the students and often visited us.

There was Prof. Dawid Bosch of University of South Africa, who advocated for a more holistic, contextual, and Christ-centered approach to mission, who was committed to contextual theology, the role of culture in mission, and emphasized that mission is not merely about church expansion or conversion, but about participating in God's transformative work in the world. He often invited people who had a mutual concern for our country for discussions at his home. We shared our pain and concerns, supported each other's callings, and prayed together. Then there was Beyers Naude, whom I knew from childhood. He, Ben Marais, and my father studied together at Stellenbosch; they were like-minded and remained in contact. Oom Bey (Uncle Bey) established the Christian Institute, an ecumenical and nonracial organization, as a compassionate voice for justice, reconciliation, and equality. In 1977 the apartheid government placed him under house arrest for seven years.

PROTESTING INJUSTICE—FROM GUARDIANSHIP TO OWNERSHIP

After graduating, I accepted a call as a missionary to Tshilidzini, which means "place of grace," in the far north of South Africa. Tshilidzini was a "mission station" that included a hospital and a school for the physically disabled in Venda, an "independent" country under the "homeland" policies of the apartheid government.

As a result of the "mission revival" in the Dutch Reformed Church (DRC) from 1955 to 1963, a renewed commitment to mission developed in the Northern Transvaal synod, which now called itself the "Mother Church." By 1960, six new mission stations and four hospitals had been established, fourteen missionaries were in full-time service, and the missionary staff increased from four in 1956 to forty-seven in 1960. Missionaries and local evangelists were called, sent, and paid by the Mother Church.

Tshilidzini was one of the new "mission stations," established in 1956 by Rev. Nico Smith and his wife, Ellen Faul, a medical doctor who started the hospital. At that stage, it was an action *for* the people but not necessarily *with* the people and was strongly influenced by the ideology of apartheid. About forty years later, Nico Smith wrote,

> I was totally unaware of being swept up in the spirit of that time, which let me follow the great triumphant march of Apartheid, unafraid. God's will was Apartheid . . . I was not yet able to realise that the apartheid ideology had me in tow . . . that I was a coworker of the government, directly and indirectly!"[7]

This was the context into which I arrived at Tshilidzini.

In those days the DRC had been strongly influenced by an Anglican missionary strategist, Henry Venn, who proposed that

7. Smith, *Tshilidzini*, 51.

churches resulting from foreign "missionary work" should become independent and self-sustaining "indigenous" churches. Venn argued that these, like the New Testament churches, should be self-supporting, self-governing, and self-propagating. *Self-government* emphasized the autonomy of churches to make decisions and establish leadership structures rooted in their cultural context through local leaders. *Self-propagation* emphasized autonomous methods of spreading the gospel, such as storytelling, music, and community engagement, and by initiating and managing evangelism, discipleship, and church planting through local resources. *Self-support* underscored churches' reliance on their own resources for sustenance and growth, rather than external funding. Venn highlighted how indigenous churches needed to move away from depending on missionary leadership and funding. A fourth *self-* was later suggested by David Bosch, *self-theologizing*. The four "selfs" were viewed as church leaders' best practice, to do what would be sustainable and culturally appropriate.

Unfortunately, these "selfs" did not always happen. Financial support was often still provided or at least supplemented by foreign money. In addition, by controlling finances, "missionaries" remained the voice of authority on many levels. Mission churches were frequently prevented from determining their own local church structures to reflect their local needs and values.

The DRC supported the policy of apartheid and worked closely with the South African government. In turn, the apartheid regime supported rural "mission outreach," but it would not subsidize "mission work" as such and rather supported the church to negotiate sites for mission stations, schools, and hospitals, and to finance hospitals and educational institutions.[8]

We arrived in Tshilidzini in 1972, uninformed about the history, worldview, traditions, or culture of the mission. It had a large membership, twenty "outposts," seven evangelists, a three-hundred-bed hospital, and a school for the disabled, all financed externally. I realized that this ministry was not self-sustainable. I did not know what was expected of me, where to fit in, to whom

8. Crafford, *Aan God die dank*, 292.

and how to be accountable. I became aware of uneasiness and irritation among some local leaders and youth leaders about the powers of church and state. *How could I and should I encourage self-determination?* The importance of the "selfs" was clear, but *how* to facilitate the process was my challenge. All of this was in the context of growing resistance against apartheid and patriarchy. Power struggles, racism, confrontation, protest, and mistrust dominated the community.

Four years after arriving at Tshilidzini, 1976 was a traumatic year. In the Soweto Youth Uprising of June 16, thousands of students protested the Bantu Education Act of 1953, which institutionalized inferior education for black South Africans. They also marched against Afrikaans as a medium of instruction in schools. The peaceful protests in Soweto escalated countrywide. Heightened political activism and civil unrest included attacks on symbols of apartheid and institutions associated with it. The Black Consciousness Movement and organizations like the South African Students Organisation, raised political awareness among students. These events transformed the social and political landscape in South Africa and contributed to increased resistance against oppressive apartheid policies.

As student protests spread countrywide, nothing was spared. Tshilidzini became a community of distrust, polarization, fear, and anger. In Venda, schoolchildren initiated mass protests—schoolbooks were burned, and schools were closed. I recall driving out of the church premises adjacent to the hospital entrance, only to be confronted with a protest march against racial discrimination at the hospital. I was caught between rival factions. On the one side were police and the hospital superintendent, on the other, the protesters. Although I was also part of the hospital management, my sympathy lay with the protesters. *Who and what did I truly represent in the eyes of the community?*

On Wednesday, June 23, 1976, while visiting family in Pretoria, I received a telephone call from our mission secretary: "The church is burning!" I decided to return to Tshilidzini and drove through the night, accompanied by my father and brother-in-law. On our arrival, we were confronted with shocked, disillusioned, and traumatized congregants, and the smouldering remains of what had been the church building. We later learned that the church had become a targeted symbol of apartheid.

The church, which had seated four hundred people, was designed in the style of a large, traditional Venda hut with Venda cultural symbols painted on the outer walls and Christian symbols on the inner walls. The bell tower was in the form of a beckoning hand, inviting people to worship, with a prominent cross in the opening. The internal layout had its own symbolism. An outside circle was reserved for visitors, nonmembers, and nonbelievers. The baptismal font was placed at the entrance to the inner circle, symbolizing that after conversion, the believer had to be baptized into the circle of believers. Significantly, there was also a separate area designated "Whites Only."

It had been customary to commence each day with a prayer meeting for hospital, church, and mission staff. Attendance was usually about eighty people. The morning after the fire, approximately three hundred people turned up, standing around the smouldering ashes of the church, shocked, confused, and afraid, singing softly, praying, and worshiping God. *Why did this happen? What was the message of the arsonists?*

My message was from Rom 8:31–39, which included these words of Paul the apostle:

> Who shall separate us from the love of Christ? Shall trouble or hardship or persecution or famine or nakedness or danger or sword? . . . No, in all these things we are more than conquerors through him who loved us. For I am convinced that neither death nor life, . . . neither the present nor the future, nor any powers . . . will be able to separate us from the love of God that is in Christ Jesus our Lord. (Rom 8:35–39)

One person after another prayed with deep piety. "Father, teach us to understand what we must learn from these things" was the refrain in many of the prayers. We also prayed the Apostles' Creed in closing.

Being with my shocked faith community and confessing our dependence on God amid the smoking ashes, was a solidarity that superseded the experiences of injustice. A women's prayer meeting in the church was scheduled for 3 p.m. on Thursdays. Because there was no longer a church, the women gathered on the lawn at the parsonage. They sat with bowed heads while one woman read from the Bible. After a few prayers, a nurse stepped forward, took my hand, and said, "We must not weep; it is a matter for the Lord—trust him!"

In the following days we experienced confusion and grief, but also a spirit of compassion, reconciliation, transformation, and hope—a new community stood in the ashes, with loyalty, care, and support. Our community voiced its pain about an unjust and racially divided society, and demonstrated the power of God's love, compassion, and reconciliation as an answer to violence, hatred, and polarization. Symbols of discrimination, of believers versus nonbelievers, and the "Whites Only" pews, were all destroyed. At the first church service in the ruins of the fire, these practices had ceased, never to be reintroduced! The hospital matron, reflecting on events, commented, "The burning of the church was a devastating experience. And yet something positive came from it."

In the following days and months, I witnessed a powerful regrouping of the faith community. A church member pointed to the cross in the church tower, that the horizontal bar of the cross, symbolizing our relationships, had been destroyed by the fire, but that the vertical bar representing our relationship with God, was still safely in place, adding, "Even though they succeeded in destroying the church building, they could not destroy the Christ of the church. Look! The crosses painted on the inner wall have also remained intact!" This became a metaphor for our challenges as Christ's followers—to rediscover and re-author our relationships with one another in our context and the political context and tensions of the time.

I realized that this was "local theology," a community with knowledge, wisdom, and skills creating local meaning that would take us forward. This was just the first of many testimonies:

- "I believe that through the burning of the church, many people have been spiritually strengthened," said a congregant.
- "We must pray for those who burnt the church, that they may also experience the peace of God that passes all understanding," said a Sunday school child.
- A cancer patient with six children and a pension of nineteen rand per month, gave one rand, saying, "I wish I could give more."
- A Teacher: "God's cause will not suffer with this event . . . on the contrary, something new awaits us!"
- A visiting pastor: "People can protest, even participate in violence and arson . . . but in the end, we must still sit down, listen, talk, negotiate, and reconcile."
- Visitors from a distant congregation arrived, announcing, "We are here to help clean up."

The following Sunday, worshipers and visitors from different denominations gathered under the trees next to the ruins. The message was from Phil 1:12: "I want you to know, brothers and sisters, that what has happened to me has really served to advance the gospel." One of the visitors affirmed, "These events must carry us across our differences of race, color, and prejudice, into a new fellowship into the Body of Christ. Together we must explore God's plan for us in our local community."

Grounded in human experience, 2 Cor 5:16–18 describes a spirituality of inclusivity that transcends polarization and becomes an invitation to reconciliation.

> So from now on we regard no one from a worldly point of view. Though we once regarded Christ in this way, we do so no longer. Therefore, if anyone is in Christ, the new creation has come: The old has gone, the new is here! All this is from God, who reconciled us to himself through Christ and gave us the ministry of reconciliation.

The fire became a powerful metaphor in our conversations: "What did the fire want to destroy in our perceptions of one another?

What traditions and apartheid practices were destroyed? Was God present in the same way as in the burning bush in Exod 3? What was God's message? What did the fire purify, as in Mal 3:3? In what way did the fire open new pathways for us to explore?"

The church council met the following Saturday to discuss the events and challenges, searching for a way ahead. "What now? Who should be blamed? What should be our message to the congregation and the community?" Voices of anger, revenge, reconciliation, forgiveness, love, and opportunity marked the challenges of a new beginning. We unpacked what forgiveness would mean in our present situation. "Did it mean accepting the situation and simply releasing the perpetrators? If we did not forgive, would it mean that we were prisoners of our own circumstances?" We learned that forgiveness is powerful and liberating if we let go and did not carry the pain and grief with us. Forgiveness was more about us than the arsonists. Alan Paton said,

> It is not "forgive and forget" as if nothing wrong had ever happened, but forgive and go forward, building on the pain of the past and the energy generated by reconciliation, to create a new future.[9]

But such forgiveness also entails responsibility towards perpetrators, to love, understand, reconcile, and set them free.

During the lunch break, a senior church council member called me aside. He diplomatically explained that in many African cultures, "loyalty is more important than the truth." Suddenly, my perspective and understanding were under scrutiny. *What did he mean? What had I missed? Whose loyalty was at stake? What about the truth? What was his loyalty? What was his truth? What was his message to me? What were my loyalties and my truths? On whose side was justice?*

In this context, I learned that loyalty implies faithfulness and committed support to a person, a group, or a faith community. It is about being reliable and consistent in commitment, even during challenging times. Loyalty can foster trust, emotional security, and

9. Paton, *Cry*, 79.

strong interpersonal bonds, making it a foundational element in personal relationships and in the body of Christ. In addition, I was discovering that truth is about honesty, accuracy, and integrity, the foundation of transparent communication and informed decision-making. Upholding truth is crucial for accountability and justice, and it may sometimes conflict with loyalty, especially when loyalty might require withholding the truth or being complicit in deception.

The elder's point was that truth would expose the transgressors and make them enemies and culprits who were punishable. But we did not know what their circumstances were. "Was it possible that the arsonists were committed to fighting apartheid and injustice and that they had mistakenly chosen the wrong target? Were they not also loyal to their truth?" The elder's plea was not to allow our different truths to collide, and create further polarization, but to be loyal to our chosen commitment as Christians, to work towards restoration, reconciliation, and common loyalty. Pursuing truth was not about prosecuting individuals but had to be focused on a community process of gathering evidence, to rebuild relationships and trust between individuals and groups, for healing and reconciliation. It involved acknowledging past wrongs, addressing the needs of victims, and promoting a shared commitment to human rights, to prevent future violence and fear.

The elder was, in a diplomatic way, explaining the presence of *ubuntu*—that ubuntu was trying to direct our experience and meaning-making. I was learning that somebody with ubuntu is relational, inclusive, generous, hospitable, friendly, caring, forgiving, and compassionate. Archbishop Desmond Tutu wrote that ubuntu means "my humanity is caught up, is inextricably bound up, in theirs. . . . I am human because I belong."[10] Ubuntu fosters a sense of belonging, mutual support, and a common loyalty above differences. It creates space for forgiveness, reconciliation and healing and opens space to move forward from past injustices.

The church council unanimously accepted the situation as their responsibility and decided to build a new church building as soon as possible. It was their opportunity to re-author their identity

10. Tutu, *No Future Without Forgiveness*, 64.

and claim their agency. The indigenous style of the old church associated with apartheid's ideology of "separate development" was in ashes. Now an opportunity arose to create a structure that had a message of reconciliation and unity in Christ. A new period slowly emerged. The congregation migrated from a "mission" situation, where important decisions were made by missionaries and outside supporting bodies influenced by apartheid structures, to a spiritually responsible community of believers, exercising their agency. I was no longer a "missionary" sent by the Mother Church but a minister and colleague, in service of and accountable to the church council.

Two weeks later it was Holy Communion. It rained so much that we had to assemble in a ward at the hospital for the main service. The congregants sat on the floor as we shared the bread and wine from a few mugs, as our communion tableware had been destroyed. This was a reminder that nothing tangible survived the heat of the fire; even the granite baptismal font had crumbled into fragments. The sermon was taken from 1 Cor 3:8–20.

> For we are partners working together for God . . . you are also God's building, and the Holy Spirt dwells in you . . . God has already placed Jesus Christ as the only foundation, and no other foundation can be laid . . . but each one must be careful how he builds. (Paraphrased)

For the next two years while we planned and built the new church, we worshiped in a tent, a stone's throw from the ruins. It was an in-between time of "no more" and "not yet," a liminal time of transition, a landscape with no discernible road map. Richard Rohr says of such times, "This is a good space where genuine newness can begin . . . it is God's waiting room."[11] In my experience, this incident was a sacred space of pilgrimage through grief and mourning, towards wholeness and hope, even during uncertainty—an act of faith. I experienced in this pilgrimage of liminality a new ownership of our spirituality—a period of rediscovering our stewardship as disciples of Christ, and our calling to reconciliation

11. Rohr, *Everything Belongs*, 155–56.

as witnesses to his love. It was a period of calling on Christ's help and re-authoring our identity, before we were ready to rebuild the church building.

During this time, I contracted jaundice and was hospitalized for three months. My experience was that I had been taken out of the situation so that the church council could take the initiative and continue rebuilding in my absence. I was learning to create space for local autonomy and creativity. Their planning, funding, and building of the new church was a challenging but also a rewarding experience. The physical building became a metaphor for a community of believers who took agency in building their own relationship with God with a spirituality that rose above race, social upheaval, conflict, tradition, and polarization.

On August 19, 1979, the new church was inaugurated—planned and built mostly by church members. It was a time of ecumenical celebration, owning our own creation, and making meaning. We celebrated a newfound *koinonia*. The inscription on the commemoration plate read:

> "The glory of this present house will be greater than the glory of the former house," says the Lord Almighty. "And in this place, I will grant peace," declares the Lord Almighty. (Hag 2:9)

BRINGING INJUSTICE INTO A CONTEMPLATIVE CONVERSATION

As a pastoral narrative therapist with hindsight on such traumatic events and years, how do I revisit and reflect on those stories of resurrection and reconciliation? What has been my approach? What were my mistakes, and what may I take forward? I have realized that this was a pilgrimage towards hope and trust, motivated by my relationship with Compassion, which has accompanied me throughout my years. Compassion accompanied me out of a dominant abusive narrative of "no more," through an uncharted liminal landscape, to the alternative empowering narrative of "what now?" We, together as a new community of believers, as the body of Christ, had traveled:

- from isolation to relationships
- from exclusion to inclusion
- from fear/distrust to trust
- from grief to healing
- from subjugation to ownership
- from being voiceless/silenced to claiming our own voice
- from injustice to restorative justice
- from disillusionment to hope
- from being silent to witnessing
- from prejudice to appreciation and compassion
- from brokenness to wholeness
- from confrontation to reconciliation, communion, and freedom

In narrative therapy terms, these statements may be described as *unique outcomes* contribute to developing rich *alternative stories* that empower and create. Stories of confrontation with so many faces of injustice and grief now contributed to a re-authoring, a new identity of wholeness in Christ. These *alternative stories* can be seen as different colored threads interweaving a tapestry of wholeness.

A spirituality of wholeness in Christ weaves various aspects of one's being into a meaningful relationship with God. It involves recognizing and embracing the interconnectedness of all of life, aligning oneself with purpose, in a relationship with God that transcends dominant, abusive discourses in one's life. It is a mindfulness that is fully present in the moment with God. It finds meaning and fulfillment in life through a deep connection with God, and honors the authenticity of every individual to co-construct a living relationship with God.

The Hebrew word *shalom* has taken on a new meaning for me. It is now much more than the absence of conflict. Although translated as "peace," its meaning is much richer. It encompasses wholeness, completeness, and well-being. It is about God's will for peace and wholeness, aligning every aspect of our lives, leading to a sense of fulfillment. Shalom implies a desire for trust and communion, compassion, respect, and fulfillment, for us as individuals, our relationships, and the community. Psalm 23 says, "And I will be at home in the house of the Lord."

Dear Compassion,

Reflecting on my experiences during the uprising and burning of the Tshilidzini sanctuary, I discovered your presence in a new way. I became aware of my own uncertainty and vulnerability, of my need for you to be present. Henri Nouwen says about you,

> *Compassion is not an individual character trait, a personal attitude, or a special talent, but a way of living together . . . a compassionate life is a life in the community.*[12]

Nouwen then quotes Phil 2:1–2 to illustrate the nature of our relationship:

> *Therefore if you have any encouragement from being united with Christ, if any comfort from his love, if any common sharing in the Spirit, if any tenderness and compassion, then make my joy complete by being like-minded, having the same love, being one in spirit and of one mind.*

This I knew cognitively but have now experienced.

Practicing your presence and experiencing our common ground in your presence contributed to our loyalty to one another, transcending individual truths and present circumstances. Nouwen concludes by saying,

> *Compassion is the mind of Christ that gathers us together in community.*[13]

12. Nouwen, *Compassion*, 50.
13. Nouwen, *Compassion*, 50.

In this sense, the circumstances of our life at Tshilidzini were then another manifestation of the "mind of Christ."

I have experienced your presence as care, concern, respect, reconciliation, love, and willingness to venture into landscapes of uncertainty. You made me aware of how inconsiderate and even disrespectful I may have been towards the older pioneer missionary staff members on our team, and that I did not acknowledge their uncertainty, pain, and how they had to reposition themselves during that time of liminality and upheaval. They were people who had also responded to your call to mission, who helped plan and build the old church, long before my tenure, and who, in their understanding and experience of the context, were doing what they believed resonated with the local community.

> *Therefore, if anyone is in Christ, the new creation has come: The old has gone, the new is here! All this is from God, who reconciled us to himself through Christ and gave us the ministry of reconciliation: that God was reconciling the world to himself in Christ, not counting people's sins against them. And he has committed to us the message of reconciliation. We are therefore Christ's ambassadors, as though God were making his appeal through us. We implore you on Christ's behalf: Be reconciled to God. (2 Cor 5:17–20)*

Towards the end of 1976, I was invited by Michael Cassidy of African Enterprise to attend the Pan African Leadership Assembly in Nairobi. The purpose was to bring together African church leaders, missionaries, and evangelists to address critical issues facing the church in Africa. The assembly was attended by 737 delegates from forty-eight African countries. It was one of the highlights of my life to be able to pray with African believers, dream about the African church, and reconnect with the leaders of the East African Revival whom I met in Malawi fifteen years previously; to rediscover that we had so much in common, and that we needed each other. But I also became aware of the tensions, political violence, and poverty throughout Africa. I was invited to speak at a meeting of the Student Christian Movement at the University of Nairobi.

Being white, and probably representing apartheid in their minds, I expected a critical and possibly aggressive audience, only to be welcomed as a brother in Christ. I could share our country's pain, tensions, uncertainties, and concerns, to an audience of compassionate witnesses who wanted to understand and pray for us. The response from one of the students was, "We must stop criticizing South Africa from a distance; we should pray for your country and keep in contact." South Africans returned inspired, and because of the event, three years later, in 1979, a follow-up South African Leadership Assembly was held in Pretoria with a few thousand delegates.

Hosting a multiracial assembly in apartheid South Africa was a unique event. Listening to one another's stories and the pain of a racially divided country, worshiping together, and committing ourselves to each other, was inspiring. The delegates were challenged to return home and organize regional leadership assemblies. Back in Venda, I contacted church and community leaders, and we started organizing a local Zoutpansberg Leadership Assembly, only for it to be banned by the Venda Government. I learned later that they suspected we were planning to organize the churches throughout Venda to protest Venda's independence. An opportunity to reach out, have fellowship, and experience the body of Christ in Africa was lost.

According to the Promotion of Bantu Self-Government Act 46 of 1959, black people were classified into ethnic groups for whom separate national states, called Homelands or Bantustans, were created. Many people living in South Africa were relocated. Venda was granted partial self-governance in 1973, and the apartheid regime replaced authentic community leaders with incompetent, easily manipulated traditional chiefs as intermediaries for indirect white apartheid rule. In 1979, South Africa proclaimed Venda an independent republic.

During the late 1970s the political situation in Venda was volatile. Many Venda people resisted the Homeland policy as an imposition of "independence" and a ploy to legitimize apartheid and maintain white supremacy. Discontent among the youth and the churches led to protests. The authorities responded with violence. Clergy and lay church leaders played a crucial role in opposing Venda's "independence" as part of the broader struggle against apartheid in the Black Consciousness Movement and the Student Christian Movement.

A Venda student uprising, second in magnitude only to the Soweto uprising of 1976, demonstrated the youth's determination and anger. Many were detained under the Internal Security Act for up to ninety days without trial. In October 1981, the Sibasa Police Station in Venda was bombed by uMkhonto weSizwe (MK). Several police officers were killed. However, the Venda authorities assumed that the attack was orchestrated by "revolutionaries" within Venda, and so arrested twenty-three local community leaders, among them four church leaders who had a strong following in Venda. Tshenuwani Farisani and Tshifhiwa Ike Muofhe were among those arrested.

Farisani was a South African politician, theologian, and Lutheran minister. During apartheid, he was one of the most prominent black clergy preaching liberation theology from his diocese in Venda and Transvaal. He and Muofhe cofounded the Black Evangelical Youth Organisation with Cyril Ramaphosa in the early 1970s. Farisani was active in the Black Consciousness Movement, especially as president of the Black People's Convention, from 1973 to 1975.[14] He was arrested on four occasions. During the uncertainty before his arrest, Beyers Naudé visited the two of us. I was touched by Naudé's compassion and pastoral approach, that he traveled all the way from Johannesburg to be with us. The opportunity to share, discuss the situation, and pray together was a relief, an inspiration, and an encouragement that carried me.

14. Editor's note: In what follows, Farisani is sometimes referred to as "Dean Farisani" because he became dean of his diocese in the Evangelical Lutheran Church of South Africa. As our manuscript was contracted for publication, we were saddened to hear of the death of Tshenuwani Farisani, on May 29, 2025. A parliamentary eulogy about his contribution to the struggle for justice under apartheid can be read at Parliament of the Republic of South Africa. See, "Parliament Mourns."

I met Tshifhiwa Muofhe shortly after my arrival in Venda in February 1974. He and a close friend, Laurence Khorombi, welcomed us on behalf of the wider ecumenical faith community in Venda. As a white Afrikaner, inexperienced, uncertain, and not knowing the language and the culture, I felt accepted and invited into a wider community of believers. Tshifhiwa often came in the evenings at my request and helped me with my Venda language studies. This, for me, was the beginning of a long, enriching companionship and mentorship.

Towards the end of 1979, we discussed his pending marriage to Lillian Tendani Rasengani. He wanted a bachelor party and wedding ceremony with a very clear Christian character. The bachelor party took the form of a discussion on the "meaning and responsibilities of a Christian marriage." I was asked to introduce the topic of a Christian marriage for half an hour, then he chaired the discussion that followed, until late into the night. A year later Tshifhiwa and Lillian joined us on a marriage enrichment course for ten days. They were the only black couple and integrated happily into the group. It was an experience of how reconciliation, trust, and Christian love could unify us through Christ. The commitment with which the young man experienced his relationship with Jesus Christ, and the way in which he spoke to it, touched me.

Tshifhiwa was actively involved in various Christian organizations like the Student Christian Movement in high schools, the University Christian Movement, and the Zoutspansberg Independent Ministers Association. He was also a founding member of Bold Evangelical Christian Organization (BECO), an organization that aimed to introduce people to Christ, and to strengthen Christians to remain faithful to Christ and the church. BECO encouraged ecumenical fellowship and social responsibility, and voiced opposition to injustice.

Even though Lutheran priests had no involvements with MK contacts, all were detained and tortured in prison. On November 12, 1981, Tshifhiwa Muofhe died, two days after being arrested. The authorities attempted to conceal the circumstances around his death. However, eyewitness accounts gathered by the Truth and

Reconciliation Commission concluded that "he was killed by torture while in police custody."[15] These human realities in the Sibasa police station bombing are significant in South Africa's history of resistance, violence, and the struggle for justice during apartheid.

Recently, many years after Lillian passed away, I decided to write her a letter as an opportunity for self-reflection, to revisit past experiences and how they contributed to a continuous authoring of my life and identity, and to reflect on how I was touched by her resilience and trust in God in these trying times:

Dear Lillian,

We remained in contact for many years after your beloved Tshifhiwa was killed by the Venda security police. We talked about Tshifhiwa, but I now have this need to talk to you—to revisit our time together. His death and the surrounding circumstances have influenced our lives in a profound way. You lost a husband, Mulanga lost her father, I lost a friend and mentor, the community and the church lost a dynamic leader and a voice of Christian love and re-conciliation, a voice against the injustices of apartheid and the Venda regime.

We had so much in common: our relationship with Christ, our calling to evangelize, our participation in ecumenical relationships, our joint concern about political developments in our country, and our opposition to the abusive practices of apartheid. Tshifhiwa also introduced me to two Venda Bible translators, Rev. Farisani and Mr. Mahamba.

You will recall that we attended a ten-day life revision and marriage enrichment course as two couples, in 1981, with eight other couples, facilitated by Hans Bürki, a Swiss theologian from the International Fellowship of Evangelical Students. In those days it was unheard of, even unlawful, to organize and attend multiracial gatherings. In your book, And We Forgave Them, *you recall:*

> *God has His way of putting the right people in place long before anything happens because He is omniscient. A year before his death, Tshifhiwa and I had gone to a marriage*

15. Philpott, "Death of Tshifhiwa Muofhe," 245.

> *enrichment course. We were the only black couple at the conference, but many wonderful and loving Christians surrounded us. Among them was a person from Pretoria who became very instrumental in helping me to get excellent lawyers. I owe the Louws my gratitude for inviting us to the conference, because Tshifhiwa and I unknowingly made contacts which became beneficial during the darkest hours of my life. It was a safe space for all of us to be open and vulnerable to share our pain, but also to experience how reconciliation, trust and Christian love could reconcile us in Christ.*[16]

As far as I remember, Tshifhiwa, Cyril Ramaphosa, Laurence Khorombi, and Peter Phaswana founded the Bold Evangelical Christian Organization with the message "Preaching the stable gospel to an unstable world." I was invited to speak at their gatherings and felt privileged when they invited me to serve on the Panel of Reference with Dean Farisani. I now openly identified myself with an organization that was radically preaching justice, reconciliation, and hope in the face of apartheid repression.

Then, on the night of October 26, 1981, the Sibasa police station was targeted and bombed. The bombing stunned everybody; the community was in a state of shock and polarized. A state of confusion followed. The Venda government, the police, and the security cluster were caught off guard—they panicked, responded in desperation, and started to arrest people indiscriminately. Early on November 12, 1981, I received a phone call from your sister, Munjadziwa, informing me that Tshifhiwa had been arrested, only to learn the next day from Dr. Teichler's wife, that Tshifhiwa had died in custody. My impression was that the Venda officials wanted to conceal his death out of fear of further violence. The family was expected to remain under the impression that he was still in detention until they were to be informed. Dr. Teichler and I agreed that by remaining silent, we would be tacit partners with corruption and injustice. We decided, irrespective of the risks, to visit you and inform you. On our way, we went to your pastor, Rev. Mahamba, who also had not heard the

16. Muofhe et al., *And We Forgave Them*, 83.

news. The three of us then visited you, and Rev. Mahamba spoke—we just sat in silence. I later fetched Munjadziwa to be with you.

Your experience of loss and grief was intense and painful to witness. As the news spread, it became a community grief, silently protesting injustice.

The days before the funeral were very challenging. There were roadblocks. I was stopped by the police, ordered to get out of my car, interrogated, and threatened in the presence of my family. The day before the funeral, I assisted two Lutheran pastors to secretly escape from Venda, and later that day, I collected their wives to transport them out of Venda to safety. I was later visited by the security police because they suspected that I was hiding Rev. Mahamba. People's trust was frayed—who was on whose side? Who witnessed what? Who were the perpetrators? Who were the victims? It was a community in shock.

I helped plan and organize the funeral. The security police intervened. Political parties wanted to exploit the event ideologically. The Venda government was not interested in your or the family's loss and grief. They merely wanted to restore their image to the outside world. In the meantime, Dean Farisani, Rev. Mahamba, and Rev. Phaswana were also detained and tortured. Some relatives wanted a traditional burial, but you were adamant that it should be a Christian funeral with a strong, clear message about God's grace and inclusive love. We had to negotiate with the authorities for an autopsy and for the release of Tshifhiwa's body so the funeral could take place. For me, it was a time of uncertainty, and we had to make many decisions on the spur of the moment.

On the day of the funeral, some of the prominent guests you had invited were intercepted at roadblocks and prevented from attending. The church was packed, probably between seven hundred and eight hundred people. Rev. Phaswana officiated. He read from Exod 20:13, "You shall not murder," and then also from the summary of the law in Matt 22:37–40, "Love your neighbor as yourself" (v. 39). His message in fact addressed the state about the murder, hence his theme: "You shall not kill." To those present, he said that our answer to the events is, "We must love one another," a challenging message of reconciliation. The funeral itself was a testimony of God's compassion, love, and reconciliation, but also a call for justice. Lillian, you had the admiration of all of us. You were calm, refused to wear black, and took some pictures at the grave. Everyone went home, and there was no traditional meal after the funeral. The support of the community, and more widely, was a testimony to your and Tshifhiwa's commitment to serve God and to work towards wholeness, reconciliation, and peace.

Two weeks after Tshifhiwa's burial, you were interrogated by the Venda police, and they tried to convince you to become a state witness. They said, "If you become a state witness, you will be protected and free of harassment. Think about it. You tell us something about Tshifhiwa, and you can earn money." We realized then that you urgently needed legal counsel. That evening, we secretly drove you out of Venda. You later wrote,

> *I slipped out of Venda and went to Pretoria . . . we were stopped at a roadblock, but they did not recognize me . . . I think they thought I was a nanny to the Louws. . . . I felt a sense of victory over the forces of evil that wanted to mutilate my spirit.*[17]

Thinking back on my journey with you, Matt 9:36 gives voice to my experience at the time; it reads:

> *When [Jesus] saw the crowds, he had compassion on them, because they were harassed and helpless, like sheep without a shepherd.*

To paraphrase this verse in the context of our experience, "When Jesus saw you in your grief and pain, He was deeply moved with pity; you were harassed, bewildered, helpless, vulnerable, and exposed to the abusive, violent practices of the powers of darkness." But in your own words, you were not without your shepherd; you said, "Life was never the same after my husband was killed in prison. But I never lost my faith in God. Through those difficult times in my life, I have found solace in my faith in God and His promises. I wouldn't have

17. Muofhe et al., *And We Forgave Them*, 140.

made it on my own without His guidance, grace, and love. He is still my rock in everything."[18]

I would like to share with you from Daniel Migliore's book Reading the Gospels with Karl Barth, *where Migliore considers Barth's reflection on the "compassion" of Jesus Christ.*[19]

The context is when Jesus saw the crowds and had compassion for them, a visceral experience. The Greek word "splanchna," for compassion, literally means the entrails—one's bowel—and in this context, refers to the seat of the emotions. The equivalent for us is to speak of the heart as the seat and source of love, sympathy, and mercy.

Migliore writes:

> *The misery that was before Him not only affected Him, not only touched His heart—but entered His heart, into His very being . . . it was now completely His: He suffered it in their place. The human Jesus is the perfect image of God, He shows forth the compassion of God in the proclamation and realisation of the kingdom of God as its attendant blessings of peace and reconciliation. Karl Barth said: "The person of Jesus is the royal human being, in so far as He is not only one human being with other human beings, but the human being for them: just as God is for them—the human being, in whom the love, faithfulness, salvation and glory of God is directed to them . . . He is . . . the work and the revelation of the compassion of God, of God's Gospel, Kingdom of peace and reconciliation . . . He is, in this sense, God's creaturely, earthly, human correspondence."*[20]

I was also moved by the questions: How can we creatively respond to Jesus' call to "Be compassionate just as your Heavenly Father is compassionate?" (Luke 6:36, CEB) How can we make compassion the source of our lives? Where can God's compassionate presence become visible in everyday lives? How is it possible for us, broken and sinful human beings, to follow Jesus, to become manifestations

18. Muofhe et al., *And We Forgave Them*, 143.

19. Migliore, *Reading the Gospels*, 163.

20. Migliore, *Reading the Gospels*, 131.

of God's compassion? What does it mean for us to enter solidarity with our fellow human beings and offer them obedient service? And a related question I am asking is: Who is the crowd today that is harassed and helpless like sheep without a shepherd?

In a letter you once wrote to me, you said,

> *It is hard to be a widow, but harder still, is to be a widow of a man loved by thousands, when that man was Tshifhiwa, young and intelligent, brave, a lover of people, a man who feared God, the burden is sometimes unbearable. The whole drama of his death seems utterly unreal. It hurts so much, that one wonders where God is when it hurts. As a child of God, I'm walking in darkness now, and I have no light. I am surrounded by the darkness of trouble and perplexity. But I know that the Lord was not spared the blackest midnight that ever fell on humankind. I know that I must defy the darkness and the devil who rules in it. I need more strength than ever, and I'm sure that this is only found through prayer, even in darkness. . . . But beloved, when all hope seems to disappear, in these times when I do not see where I am heading, I draw nigh to God, for He is near. Keep praying for me so that I do not forget that I am invited to "come near to God, and He will come near to me" (James 4:8).*

In 2018, in your book, you wrote,

> *Forgiving people after such a severe loss was hard. I was assailed by anger and bitterness . . . it was difficult for me to embrace forgiveness . . . I realised that I was on the way to destroying myself by carrying the guilt of my husband's killers. I discovered that without God it is extremely difficult . . . the word of God tells us to forgive those who have wronged us and to never seek to satisfy ourselves through revenge. However, circumstances triggered my deepest emotions, and I wanted to scream. Talking about traumatic experiences helps victims to address losses they never thought they could handle. In the end, a person must be willing, with the help of God, to forgive and open up*

> *about the traumatic experiences . . . forgiveness is necessary to live a healthy life.*[21]

Yes, dear Lillian, death ends a life but not a relationship. Thank you once again for a rich and meaningful relationship that we could experience throughout so much pain and injustice. Your vulnerability and honesty in your grief, as well as your trust in God, inspired me in my own journey towards wholeness in Christ.

I greet you.

Faure

TRANSCENDING PRISON WALLS

We got to know Munjadziwa, Lillian's younger sister, as a high school scholar. After school, she studied nursing and worked in the Tshilidzini hospital. She often visited our home and had a fun relationship with our children, sometimes with a sweet in her pocket to surprise them. We had a mutually transparent relationship, sharing our concerns about our country. Then, Munjadziwa was also detained. Her story of compassion towards her abusers is a witness to God's grace and healing, and a continuation of her sister's testimony. She was arrested by apartheid security police for her alleged anti-apartheid activism. She was interrogated and eventually sexually abused in custody. One night after she was released, she unburdened herself to my wife and me. With painful tears, we heard how she was expected to be silent, to sacrifice her conscience, her ethical position, her faith, her intellectual freedom, her right to a just and free society, and then to sacrifice her body. We were overwhelmed by her strength, spiritual integrity, peace, and serenity—a wholeness we could not fathom. I remember asking her, "How did you feel, and what did you think about those perpetrators during your humiliating ordeal?" Her answer remains with me vividly: "I looked into their eyes and could see their fear, loneliness, and lostness, and nothing to hold on to, and I then knew, for sure, I had something they did not have: a relationship

21. Muofhe et al., *And We Forgave Them*, 147–48.

with God, a life of love and freedom that was far more and beyond the confines of a cold and hostile prison cell. That kept me going. Actually, I felt sorry for them!"[22]

In Munjadziwa, we encountered a spirituality that cannot be described or taught. Her spirit and life transcended the walls of a prison cell, rising above violence and fear, liberating and leading her into peace and wholeness. We were touched by how Munjadziwa voiced her faith and compassion, despite the death of her brother-in-law and her torture. She demonstrated Phil 4:7 in action: "The peace of God, which is far beyond understanding, will keep your hearts and minds safe *in union with Christ Jesus*" (GNB, emphasis added). Munjadziwa's transcendent spirit confronted my moral outrage about apartheid injustices and impressed on me that forgiveness is not about the perpetrator as such, but about letting go of hatred and anger that keeps in bondage those who have been wronged. Migliore's insight about Jesus' visceral compassion took on new meaning; I realized that the misery of these sisters, Lillian and Munjadziwa, not only affected Christ, touching his heart, but in their misery, they *entered* his heart, his very being. Their misery was now completely his.

In the December after Tshifhiwa's death, we made a family visit to my parents in Zimbabwe. On our return in January, the children went to greet and play with their friends. Two hours after our arrival we were served with a notice from the Venda government that my work permit was revoked. We had to leave Venda immediately. With six hours to pack, we left the same evening. Now it was our turn to feel harassed, bewildered, helpless, vulnerable, and exposed. *Was this the price for being compassionate?*

We were not given a reason. We looked at each other with shock, disillusionment, grief, and many questions: *What now? Was this the end of our ministry at Tshilidzini?* Our years at Tshilidzini had been richly meaningful. We had experienced God's grace and guidance through a resurrection, out of the ashes of racial mistrust. We had ventured from paternalism to ownership and agency

22. Munjadziwa Muofhe gave the author permission to publish this part of her story.

in the congregation, the community, and our ecumenical circles, from pain and confrontation against injustices, to reconciliation, from polarization and mistrust to forgiveness, inclusiveness, trust, and wholeness. We had experienced the reality of 2 Cor 5:17–18:

> Therefore, if anyone is in Christ, the new creation has come: The old has gone, the new is here! All this is from God, who reconciled us to himself through Christ and gave us the ministry of reconciliation.

How were we to explain this "deportation" to our children, the congregants, the church council, our coworkers, Lillian, Munjadziwa, the community, and the supporting churches in Pretoria? I phoned Rev. Eddie Bruwer, our mission secretary in Pretoria, and explained. We hastily packed and left under police surveillance to Louis Trichardt, where we spent the night with Rev. Esterhuizen and his wife. The next morning, Rev. Bruwer, Prof. Fanie du Toit, and a close friend, Dons Kritzinger, arrived all the way from Pretoria to support us. To us, their support was a manifestation of practicing God's love, care, and compassion. We considered all the possibilities and then decided to travel to Pretoria where we were offered temporary accommodation with my sister and her husband.

The following day, traveling to Pretoria, grieving and uncertain, our four-year-old daughter was singing some Christmas carols, among others the well-known "Gloria in Excelsis Deo." She, of course, did not understand what she was trying to sing and rephrased it as *Gloria, gloria selfs in hierdie tye* which means "Gloria, gloria even in times like these." Instantly, my wife and I looked at one other and started to laugh—from the mouth of a four-year old we were given a new perspective on our situation and were challenged to recognize God's presence in our vulnerability, pain, and uncertainty.

Later, from Pretoria, in a letter to the Tshilidzini supporters, I wrote,

> The news of our deportation spread quickly, and many people arrived to say goodbye. Our children were very

> upset and unsure and did not understand what was happening. They were to return to school in Sibasa the next day, and suddenly, their world changed. Our friends' help and support were wonderful. Before we left, about fifteen church council members came to greet us; it was with them we had prayed after the arson, with whom we had built the new church. It was traumatic to suddenly have to leave what we had committed to for the past eight years. I was not in the right frame of mind to say goodbye and them so suddenly. We were grateful that the church council were people who could take responsibility, lead and would continue the work.

Our deportation was front-page news. Reporters speculated about the reason behind the deportation, assuming that it was probably because of my involvement with Tshifhiwa's funeral arrangements and my support to Lillian. *DRUM* magazine reported that I had said,

> I have nothing to hide. I don't feel guilty about anything I did in Venda. I would do it all again in similar circumstances. If I had not done it, I would have failed in my responsibility as a Christian and a pastor. It is not my terrain to criticise the Venda Government or any other government for that matter. But the church is the conscience of the state and must speak up when there is any form of injustice. . . . God cannot be used for the state's convenience.[23]

I was surprised how different news agencies reported these events according to their position regarding apartheid, homeland developments, racial issues, and what they regarded as just or unjust. Most Afrikaans pro–Nationalist Party newspapers emphasized the unjust way I had been treated, whereas English and opposition newspapers focused on the cruel way Tshifhiwa had been treated leading to his death.

This was a traumatic time for me as pastor, for my family, and for the Tshilidzini congregation. It was not momentary but had a

23. Motjuani, "Church Must Speak Up," 28–29.

lasting effect on everyone involved. In a way, the events colonized our lives, not remaining in the past but recurring into the present, reshaping present and future stories. *What motivates a person to set a church alight or to arrest a person and to torture him to death, or, as a police officer, to arrest a woman, interrogate her, and then rape her? What does it say about the context and community we live in, our values and expectations? What was their truth?* I wanted to protest and voice the experiences of the victims in their emotional and physical pain, their body wounds, and their loss of words. Shelly Rambo says,

> Trauma begins with an event or series of events that are too much to bear. The experience is beyond the "edge" of what is possible to perceive and respond to, beyond what we are able to include in our identities, as individuals or communities.[24]

We were disorientated and uncertain, as a family, about our immediate future. We had to find somewhere to stay so that the children could attend school. I had lost my chosen vocation, and political processes intervened, deciding my future and calling. I was uncertain whether I would have the opportunity to continue in the ministry or whether I should look for a secular job. Suddenly, I had to reorientate, and I did not know how. It was a time of loss and liminality, a time of letting go, but also a time of tentatively exploring uncharted, new landscapes.

Walter Brueggemann suggests that the Psalms can roughly be grouped into three movements or seasons that illustrate one's life journey.[25] "Psalms of Orientation" describe seasons of stability and well-being; everything makes sense. The "Psalms of Disorientation" describe seasons of uncertainty, loss, displacement, and lament, where the previous season of stability has collapsed; they focus on anguish, hurt, alienation, suffering, and even death, evoking disillusionment, dissatisfaction, self-pity, and resentment.

24. Rambo, *Spirit and Trauma*, 18.

25. Brueggemann, *Message of the Psalms*.

Finally, "Psalms of Reorientation" describe seasons of discovery and surprises, with alternatives to create new meaning.

Brueggemann's approach gave me thoughts about God moving from order through chaos to a new order. His seasons offered me a biblical "map" for re-authoring my experiences. Sometimes, I experienced all these seasons in one day. I had been unprepared to be forcibly removed from an environment where people experienced injustice, poverty, and racism, to an environment of economic privilege, where injustice and racism were everyday practices. To be removed from a community where we could be vulnerable, supportive, and united against injustice under difficult circumstances was traumatic. Indeed, in Brueggemann's terms, it was a time of disorientation.

ACCOMPANIED BY COMPASSION TOWARDS WHOLENESS AND HOPE

Three months later, despite the negative publicity, I received a call to serve the Elarduspark Dutch Reformed Church in Pretoria as pastor. Politically speaking, it was a period of escalating polarization and conflict. Security Police continued to detain and ban students, journalists, clerics, and black leaders. Guerrilla activity by the African National Congress increased markedly. Sporadic boycotting of schools and universities continued. Two hundred and sixty-four people were detained. Eighty-five were restricted under the Internal Security Act. At an emergency session in Geneva, a representative of the Lutheran World Federation reported twenty-one people detained in Venda, two of whom were believed to have died of torture. Attempts by the president of the South African Council of Churches, the Reverend Peter Storey, and Bishop Tutu to visit the detained clergymen were prevented. They could not enter Venda and were turned back. The DRC and Nederduitse Hervormde Kerk were suspended from the World Alliance of Reformed Churches because of their support for apartheid. Beyers Naudé was served with his second banning order, restricting him for a further three years. The order was the first to be served under the comprehensive new security law, the Internal Security Act of 1982, at the sole discretion of the Minister of Law and Order, and the decision could not be questioned in court.

After I accepted the call to Elarduspark, a season of reorientation dawned with new challenges and opportunities. I had to establish myself as a pastor in a new congregation with its unfamiliar traditions, expectations, and practices, in a community influenced by different sociopolitical structures. It was a challenge, a context I was not prepared for. My brief included preaching, home visitation, pastoral counseling, community outreach, and missions. My calling was unchanged, to serve God and participate in establishing the body of Christ in a broken world (Eph 4:12) by working towards justice, reconciliation, and peace. My identity remained that of a pastor, but I was now regarded a "political activist" by outside voices, and even by some radical church members who worked in the nationalist government and security services.

At that time, clouds of protest against apartheid gathered and a state of emergency was declared. A wide group of DRC members, clergy, and laity founded Reforum, an organization that aimed for a prophetic witness against apartheid, by calling the DRC to abandon its theology of apartheid, and by working to reunify the Dutch Reformed family of churches.[26] I contributed to Reforum's meetings and discussions about the ethical-theological-political context of South Africa. Participating in Reforum influenced my life profoundly. It was a community of compassion and concern—for the church and the country, and for one another in our different ministries. The outcome was an open letter published on June 9, 1982, with 123 signatories. We publicly addressed the problems in our churches and society, with special regard to reconciliation, church unity, and the prophetic calling of the church. We declared solidarity with all who suffered the injustice of apartheid. As a cosignatory, I was able to publicly state my position regarding our Venda experiences. The letter provoked turmoil in our denomination but played an important role in motivating the DRC to revisit its policy on church and society.

26. Meiring, "Reforum."

In 1985, the Kairos Document was published, initiated by mainly black South African theologians, in a powerful, theological statement that confronted the apartheid regime and urged churches to prophetic action.[27] This document was first discussed at a meeting held in Soweto in July 1985. The second edition, I endorsed. Several DRC leaders who had attended the National Initiative for Reconciliation also signed. It was named the Kairos Document after the Greek word *kairos*, which means a moment of truth, grace, and opportunity. The document described the DRC in South Africa as divided—a white church and a black church. The Kairos theologians also critiqued contrasting theologies to be found in South Africa—"State Theology" and "Church Theology." They proposed an alternative "Prophetic Theology" with a message of hope for the nation. This document, acclaimed by many but criticized by others, led to heated debate. It was the first of several statements calling for a new look at the role of the church in South Africa. Contributing to the activities of Reforum, the open letter, and the Kairos Document gave me back my voice of social, political compassion, which had been silenced by our deportation and sometimes in the new congregation in Elarduspark.

Experiences and lessons in Tshilidzini enriched my orientation and influenced my ministry in Elarduspark. As I took up pastoral duties, I became aware of my need to be equipped with a pastoral approach that is respectful, nonjudgmental, compassionate, and enabling. I was introduced to narrative therapy by Prof. Dirk Kotze, who has accompanied me in my ongoing journey. Narrative therapy holds that people live in stories created in relationships, through language. In a respectful, non-blaming approach to counseling and community work, narrative therapy honors people as the expert narrators of their own lives.[28] It views problems as separate from people, often personifying the problem, and encouraging a person or group to negotiate a new relationship with the problem. It assumes people have many skills,

27. Kairos South Africa, "Kairos Document."

28. Morgan, *What Is Narrative Therapy*.

competencies, beliefs, values, commitments, and abilities that can help them reduce the impact of problems in life. It provided me with a pastoral approach to participate ethically in the community, co-constructing the meaning of our relationships with self, others, and God.

Compassion accompanied me on this journey of reorientation, inspiring and alerting me to the spiritual, social, and emotional needs of the congregation and community regarding trauma, injustice, fear, and social and political anxiety. I became part of a team of colleagues who encouraged one another to work and serve according to our gifts. We supported one another and intentionally negotiated what the congregation's needs were. These colleague-companions identified with Christ's pathways to justice through grief, hope, and wholeness. I could share with them my way of being and my understanding of Christ's call to love and reconciliation. We complemented one other in this new context, to work towards justice, wholeness, and hope.

The following four vignettes from these years are four stories of my growing understanding of Compassion accompanying me, in my new team of colleagues, in this new environment.

COMPASSION AND THE MENTALLY UNIQUELY ABLED

One morning, a mother approached me to express her pain and struggle regarding her mentally uniquely abled daughter. They did not have the financial and emotional means to care for her. I was moved to take up the challenge. With the parents and a colleague, we started a care center with two young adults. This was the beginning of a center that now provides accommodation for fourteen and a workshop for twenty-seven people. The center and its parent association gave peace of mind as parents could support each other and plan together. For the residents, the center provided a safe community in which to interact in a spontaneous way and explore their gifts. Their vulnerability and honesty, joy, enthusiasm, loyalty, love, trust, and creativity inspired us. But it was also a challenge to navigate between the needs of the children and their parents, to find financial support, and to involve other congregations. It was painful to experience the disinterested aloofness of some, but inspiring that so many people got involved and contributed to the project. It became a community of inclusion for parents and children.

COMPASSION AND THE SEXUALLY ABUSED

In my counseling and postgraduate study in narrative therapy, I became increasingly aware of the extent of child sexual abuse, involving the abuse of trust. Once, I interviewed a client in the presence of a group of five therapists and a supervisor. The group acted as "outsider witnesses" to the therapeutic interview, to reflect and comment, contributing to a richer description of the client's story. The client, who was in her early twenties, from a very young age had been sexually abused by a family member. I was moved by her story of having kept a secret for so long. She had taken responsibility for keeping her family intact by not exposing her abuser. I often wondered what it said of this woman, that although she was the victim, she was still willing to carry the burden of her secret, to protect family relationships that were so brittle.

With her permission, I revisited the story of her therapeutic journey in counseling, in my doctoral thesis. It was my ethical responsibility to involve her in the writing and editing of my version of our journey. She coined a name, Authorese, for herself, a combination of "author" and "authorize." She felt that she reclaimed her story through this re-authoring process in therapy and would "authorize" how and by whom her story was told. In her response to the final document, she wrote,

> When I met the team, I was alone and afraid. I felt second hand and used. Consequently, I expected that other people, if they knew my story, would perceive me in the same way. To my surprise the contrary happened. I experienced *respect, warmth* and *genuineness*. This helped me to again believe in the goodness of people. In turn, it

> helped me believe in myself and that I was good enough to be loved by someone again. In the therapy, I retrieved my dignity and realised that I was venturing into new possibilities.
>
> . . . As time passed, I managed to replace the bad memories and entertained the positive and good ideas so that, in the end, the good ideas were more than the bad memories. I've also experienced God's goodness and grace. The group cared for me. They kept me warm when I was numb with cold. I will never in my life accept it is God's will that women and children should be molested and raped. Even today, I do not understand why this should have happened to me. But today, it is not so important to understand why it happened. It is far more important to know and claim that I am healed and to keep believing that God loves me and will never forsake me.
>
> Looking back on my journey, I can say that I have repossessed my life, and I know that I will not falter. I may not allow my life and myself to fall from my hands. I have worked too hard to repossess my life, and I will not let it go . . . somebody lashes out at the treasures in my hand, and if they fall in pieces on the floor, I will still hold on to *what I have got*![29]

After therapeutic sessions with Authorese concluded, we often met and reflected on her resilience, her agency in reclaiming her life, and her owning of justice for those who fell victim to sexual abuse. She later qualified in narrative therapy and contributed as a therapist to people with similar stories.

COMPASSION AND GENDER IDENTITY

Compassion accompanied me on a journey into the identity struggles of some in the LGBTQI+ community, who often face loneliness, isolation, and self-doubt, because of verbal abuse, physical violence, systemic discrimination, and rejection—a situation Tutu

29. Emphasis original.

describes as "as evil as apartheid."[30] I came to realize how many LGBTQI+ people model resilience and strength, fostering a deep empathy and compassion, and role modeling ways to advocate for justice and equality.

A student in her second year who was active in leading the church youth movement, and whose father was part of the church leadership, made an appointment to see me. Tentative and uncertain, she shared her dream to be a mother, but believing her gayness was a sin made her feel God would punish her. This was the beginning of a journey along which she confidentially disclosed her pain, uncertainty, and many concerns, not least about her parents. How could she redefine her identity in a heterosexual, patriarchal, and predominately Christian society? Later, she got married, hoping that her identity would change, only later to get divorced. Her honesty, pain, and lostness, moved me. I felt unprepared and uncertain about how to support her to author her own identity and encounter a compassionate God in whose love she could discover her identity.

A few months later, a member of our congregation who had a close relationship with Compassion conferred with me about a gay family member who was marginalized by society and at work. After sharing her concern, she suggested that we establish a support group for gay people, their families, and interested people. I gladly accepted this invitation, not knowing how we should take on this challenge. *To begin with, how would we approach the church council? Would they give permission? What would the attitudes of the other pastors be?*

To start, I invited Rev. Andre Muller, a minister of the Reforming church, to share his story with my colleagues. The priority of this denomination is to reach out to the LGBTQI+ community, since none of the mainline churches were willing to include gay members unconditionally. After many deliberations, our church council agreed to start the support group. It gathered a few times a year for about twelve years. It became an affirming and inclusive space, where people could cry, laugh, share their stories, and

30. Battle, *Desmond Tutu*, 253.

support each other. Among others, we invited a well-known radio and TV personality, who was openly gay and had experienced marginalization as a child at school, to receive Holy Communion as an act of reconciliation and restitution, to acknowledge his honest and challenging journey and give recognition to his courage to come out of the closet. For me, publicly serving him the sacrament in a gathering of about eighty people was a new profession of my faith in Jesus and a new commitment to inclusion, justice, hope, and wholeness.

It has been a privilege on four occasions to marry same-sex couples and accompany them in marriage preparation for six weeks, where they could negotiate their relationship. Participating in the baptism of a gay couple's adopted child is, for me, a demonstration of God's commitment to reach out to the child and the parents. Administering these sacraments has brought new meaning to me, as an act of inclusion into the household of God.

After I retired, the meetings discontinued, but recently this group reconvened—an initiative of the gay church members, themselves. They advertised the new meetings with a banner: "Gay and OK."

The LGBTQI+ reality was a bone of contention in the DRC and ended up in the high court in Pretoria. The court found that DRC policy against solemnizing same-sex marriages diminished the integrity of gay congregants; that it was unfair to exclude members from the full and equal enjoyment of all rights and freedoms of church membership based on sexual orientation. In 2015, the general synod decided to allow individual church councils to recognize same-sex marriages and scrapped a rule that gay ministers had to be celibate. In 2016, the synod adopted a new policy, ignoring the 2015 ruling, which the court again set aside in its conclusion that unequal treatment of people in LGBTQI+ communities constituted discrimination according to Chapter 9 of the new South African Constitution.[31] It was embarrassing that a secular court should reprimand the church for the illegality of its theological position. Even today, congregations, church circuits,

31. Gaum and Jones, *Twelve Members' Court Battle*, 508–64.

and synods are polarized. In these experiences, I have been encouraged to witness resilience and strength in the LGBTQI+ community in the face of injustice, systemic discrimination, and emotional violence.

COMPASSION AND MY PREJUDICE

Compassion, you have accompanied me from childhood. You taught me to accompany people, support them in their pain, to hear and honor their stories, in their struggles to author new meaning and direction for their lives and relationships. This was especially so in Venda, where apartheid injustices led to victimization, discrimination, violence, and death. I also experienced your gracious way of accompanying me in my personal life, to navigate my pilgrimage towards justice and wholeness.

In Pretoria, in my capacity as a pastoral narrative therapist, I experienced your presence in new ways. Previously, you gave me compassion for the victims of apartheid. Now, you taught me to have compassion for those perpetuating apartheid, using clandestine methods, like torture, extrajudicial killings and support for surrogate forces. You enabled me to see a person and listen with a compassion to their stories of pain, guilt, and regrets for planned manipulation, violence, or murders of anti-apartheid proponents, all for the sake of apartheid. Some wanted to confess. Some felt betrayed by the apartheid government. Others were guilty or angry or carried secrets. Still others needed forgiveness, or lived in isolation, with broken marriages, or had lost contact with family members and lived in fear.

A test of my understanding of compassion and forgiveness came in a pastoral consultation between Adriaan Vlok, former minister of law and order in the apartheid regime, and a group of pastoral therapists at the Institute of Therapeutic Development. He narrated his story and confessed his key role of enforcing the system of apartheid through police hit squads who kidnapped, tortured, and murdered activists. Sitting in his presence and listening to his confession, disillusionment, pain, and regrets was disturbing, moving. Then, to be asked to pray for him caught me unprepared. But this liberated me from my prejudice. I experienced God's healing presence and restoration. He had testified at the Truth and Reconciliation Commission and, in a gesture of repentance, washed the feet of the mothers and widows of ten activists who were murdered by the police after being ambushed.

Compassion, if it were not for how you carried me, my own story would probably have prevented me from listening to the practitioners of injustice. You taught me what it means to look beyond our differences and see a person behind a story, to embody forgiveness, and to listen nonjudgmentally to others' stories, even from a radically opposing standpoint.

In 1993, eleven years after we had been deported from Venda, the Tshilidzini church council requested the Venda government to revoke the withdrawal of my work permit so that they could invite us back for a "farewell" ceremony and to preach on the Sunday. My message was from Mic 6:8 (NKJV):

> He has shown you, O man, what is good;
> And what does the LORD require of you
> But to do justly, to love mercy,
> And to walk humbly with your God?

The initiative of the church council was an act of reconciliation and restitution between "mission church" and "mother church," and between church and state.[32] For my family and me, it was a healing experience.

REFLECTING ON MY JOURNEY WITH COMPASSION

Revisiting and reflecting on my life journey presented here, I became aware how Compassion encouraged me to confront oppression and injustice, stand with those who suffer, and endure the accompanying implications—criticism, isolation, and sometimes an emotional burden. The companionship of Compassion was an experience of co-authoring and a deeply reflective and reflexive

32. Modise, "Rocky Road," 5.

experience. I found inspiration in John Paul Lederach,[33] who, while discussing Ps 85, highlights how the psalmist personifies truth, mercy, righteousness, and peace. Verse 10 reads,

> Mercy and truth have met together;
> Righteousness and peace have kissed. (NKJV)

By personifying the truth, mercy, righteousness, and peace, the psalmist animates relationships, experiences, and communication, as these meet and embrace, converse and negotiate, and contribute to each other's stories and meaning-making. Likewise, in my context, to personify, meet, embrace, and negotiate with Compassion and its rich, intertwined relationship with Justice, Truth, Peace, Reconciliation, Grief, Forgiveness, Trust, and Healing, contributed to my healing, restoration and meaning-making journey.

I realized that it was often the grief others experienced—their loss, pain, and protest, that awakened Compassion and Vulnerability within me, inviting my participation towards justice, hope, and wholeness. As I experienced an emotional shift from a landscape of injustice, trauma, and grief to a transformative landscape of restoration, wholeness, hope, and meaning making, I asked for humility and a decentered position, from which I could trust that even my imperfect efforts might contribute to healing, reconciliation, and justice.

On this journey, I have discovered that it was important for me not to see or judge the practitioners of injustice as the problem, as opposition, or even as enemies. Viewing them in such a way often leads to polarization and confrontation. Instead, I have learned to personify Injustice itself, as a force separate from the individuals behind it—to preferably approach the problem as the problem rather than making human opponents the problem. This shift in perspective enabled me to sit down, sometimes literally, sometimes metaphorically, with the practitioners of injustice—not in hostility, but in a spirit of dialogue and reconciliation, to explore what we have in common rather than to be confrontational about

33. Lederach, *Journey Toward Reconciliation*, 52–62.

our differences. It has not been an easy path, but it has often been transformative.

I would like to pay tribute to and acknowledge those in my life from whom I have learned so much. Individuals of remarkable dedication, sincerity, and sacrifice who have worked tirelessly to bring God's kingdom to life here and now. It has been—and continues to be—a meaningful journey to be with them on a pilgrimage into God's love, reconciliation, and justice. Many of these individuals have endured profound pain and injustice, experiencing its weight intensely, and have borne witness to these struggles through their very lives. I think of them as team members of my Club of Life—a metaphor in narrative therapy that describes the importance of living in relationships where we together create meaning with others who are supportive and have contributed to our identity and our taking of agency in our lives.

I also want to acknowledge my wife Huma, Dons Kritzinger, Piet Meiring, and Dirk Kotze, all fellow pilgrims in our different journeys towards hope and wholeness. They acted as invited "outsider witnesses," listening, reflecting, and asking co-creating questions along my authoring and re-authoring journey towards my preferred way of living—towards justice, peace, hope, and Christ's pathways to wholeness.

Reflecting on my pilgrimage thus far, I think of my life as a tapestry woven from the threads of my experiences, values, and relationships. These threads differ in color, strength, quality, and size, but are interwoven into a tapestry. They represent my process of meaning-making. A tapestry consists of the warp and the weft. Weft threads interlace with the warp to form the complementary design or image. The relationship between warp and weft is cooperative; together, they are the final tapestry. I think of the warp as the experiences of my childhood, my formative years as a student and what I was privileged to be exposed to and could learn, my ever-evolving relationship with God, and how Compassion was an intense and central color in my tapestry. I think of the weft as later events, experiences, traumas, grief, and even deaths, represented by the darker, more painful threads that threatened to dominate the tapestry. But also in the weft, there are the stronger, colorful threads of Ps 85's Truth, Mercy, Justice, and Peace. There is also the prophet Micah's theme in this weaving, which emerges if we "do justly," "love mercy," and "walk humbly" with God. The image that most vividly emerges is that of a loving, compassionate God of mercy, reconciliation, restitution, and hope, who, through his spirit, weaves the tapestry towards wholeness. The One in whom we live, move, and find our being likewise calls us to a life of compassion, just as he is compassionate. This tapestry is unique; it represents my narrative. It cannot be copied or repeated. I remain accountable. To conclude, my payer is this:

God of love, compassion, justice, and wholeness:

Bless us with discomfort at the footprints of injustice, oppression, corruption, and exploitation in our relationships and society.

Empower us to participate in weaving love, peace, and reconciliation into a tapestry of trust, healing, growth, and freedom in Christ.

Inspire us to share our mutual vulnerability, pain, sadness, and doubt, but also our joy, faith, and hope.

Accompany us in our healing journey towards growth and wholeness, for in you we live, move, discover, and author our being.

Amen

Afterword

A Word Before the Last: God Only Knows!

John W. de Gruchy

Our lives are books of stories, some better crafted than others, but most carefully edited and self-censored for wider scrutiny. Sometimes we share chapters or paragraphs with a soul friend, eliciting comment for improving what we have written. Family, who have heard our embellished tales about growing up and moving on through our life cycle, will offer their opinions without being asked, both in jest and by way of correction. But few will know our deepest secrets, the substance of our soul, and very few, if any, will know the whole story. "God alone knows," we thankfully say without necessarily knowing what we mean.

If God is not a part of our world and lived experience then, believe it or not, we will still not have the last word. But if God, the One in whom "we live and move and have our being" (Acts 17:28), is a reality, sometimes seemingly absent, other times vibrantly present, but always the Mystery beyond knowing, then the story acquires a different tenor and texture. Especially if at times this One wrestles with us in the darkest hours and places of our lives, which, in the process, are painfully laid bare. It is then that our lives become an open book even if they remain closed to the inspection of others. Then we discover that God knows us better than we know ourselves. But, just maybe, we will also know the

God disclosed in Jesus better, for that story is also one that traverses the full gamut of being human, so that God knows our story inside out. Then it also dawns on us that God wants to bring each of our stories to completion as we journey in Christ from brokenness to healing, from rejection to acceptance, from fragmentation to wholeness.

Along this path we cherish opportunities to share and celebrate our stories of joy and acceptance in breaking bread together with our fellow travelers. But even if it remains difficult to share with all of them the extent and specifics of our brokenness and failure, maybe, having read this book, we will also be better able to join the conversation.

We may not all be prepared to follow suit and bare our souls in the same way, but it is infinitely better to do so in our own way than to repress our hurts, fears, disillusionment, and anguish until they burst into public view in moments of frustration or anger. "Where did *that* come from?" some might ask when we explode. "God alone knows," we reply in embarrassment. But perhaps deep down we also know or can guess the answer, if we have thought deeply enough to say, "God knows," even when not pushed to explain. For one thing is certain, when we say that "God knows," our stories take on new meaning. So maybe the stories recorded here will jolt us into writing the next chapter of our stories differently—perhaps less as a record of the journey of our self and more as a testimony as to its meaning, its struggles, and its direction.

I am usually reticent to share my vulnerability and weakness, though since the death of our son Steve fifteen years ago, I have shifted from the academic "we" to the personal "I" in my writing. Even so, I confess that I still prefer to tell my story my way, so that I can control the way it is heard or read, and have the last word if it were possible. But I have learned that while it is often better to remain silent and store things up in my heart than it is to blurt them out without thought, and that sharing the vagaries of my story with a trusted friend is infinitely better than bottling it up to preserve respect, I have also accepted that I will not have the last word.

The authors of this book have broken all the social norms by going public. God is not alone in knowing their stories; we have all been drawn into the intimacies and the consequences of their actions. Like fellow travelers on a *camino*, we have become part of a conversation that has the potential to change us along the way through coming to know ourselves, even as we are known by God. And clearly, that is the intention that has evoked the telling and publishing of these stories. You cannot read them and remain the same. But even if the book does not send us hastily to do likewise and tell our own stories to others with the same detail and intense honesty, maybe it has become a catalyst that helps us face ourselves as if in a mirror.

So, maybe we will decide to find a spiritual director who can help us write the next chapter in our lives better than we might have done. Maybe, by reading these stories and conversing with their authors along the way, you have already begun to live your own story differently. Maybe you are more open to the possibility that God always has more in store for each of us and that discovering and growing into God's "more" is what being Christian and becoming truly human is all about. We will never be able to write the last word, but we do have the opportunity to write the word before the last, in anticipation of the afterword that others might write. And what that is, God only knows.

Lent 2025

Bibliography

Ackermann, Denise M. *After the Locusts: Letters from a Landscape of Faith.* Cape Town: David Phillip, 2003.

Alcoff, Linda. *Visible Identities: Race, Gender, and the Self.* Oxford: Oxford: University Press, 2006.

Battle, Michael. *Desmond Tutu: A Spiritual Biography of South Africa's Confessor.* Johannesburg: Naledi, 2021.

Bonhoeffer, Dietrich. *The Cost of Discipleship.* Translated by R. H. Fuller. New York: Macmillan, 1959.

Bosch, David J. "Nothing but a Heresy." In *Apartheid Is a Heresy*, edited by John W. De Gruchy and Charles Villa-Vicencio, 75–93. London: David Philip, 1982.

Boss, Pauline. *The Myth of Closure: Ambiguous Loss in a Time of Pandemic and Change.* New York: Norton, 2021.

Botman, H. Russel. "Barmen to Belhar: A Contemporary Confessing Journey." *Nederduitse Gereformeerde Teologiese Tydskrif* 47 (2006) 240–49.

Brueggemann, Walter. *The Message of the Psalms: A Theological Commentary.* Minneapolis: Fortress, 1984.

———. *The Psalms and the Life of Faith.* Edited by Patrick D. Miller. Minneapolis: Fortress, 1995.

Butler, Samuel, trans. *The Odyssey of Homer.* London: Longmans, Green, and Co., 1898.

Christian Reformed Church. *Belgic Confession.* https://www.crcna.org/welcome/beliefs/confessions/belgic-confession.

Clarke, John G. I. "Cradock Four Inquest Judy Chalmers Testimony In Loco with Mbulelo Goniwe and Paul Verryn: Final Cut." YouTube, Jun. 6, 2025. https://www.youtube.com/watch?v=FgNc4Go3qgw&t=294s.

Coetzee, Murray H. *Die "Kritiese Stem" teen Apratheidsteologie in the Ned Geref Kerk (1905–1974): n Analise van die bydraes van Ben Marais en Beyers Naudé.* Pretoria: Bybelmedia, 2010.

Cohen, Leonard. "Democracy." *The Future.* Columbia Records, 1992.

Crafford, D. *Aan God die dank.* Pretoria: N. G. Kerkboekhandel, 1982.

De Caussade, Jean-Pierre. *The Sacrament of the Present Moment*. Translated by Kitty Muggeridge. San Francisco: HarperCollins, 1981.

Dutch Reformed Church. "Confession of Belhar (1986)." Dutch Reformed Church Archives. https://kerkargief.co.za/doks/bely/CF_Belhar.pdf.

Ellingson, Laura, and Carolyn Ellis. "Autoethnography as Constructionist Project." In *Handbook of Constructionist Research*, edited by J. A. Holstein and J. F. Gubrium, 445–65. New York: Guilford, 2002.

Ellul, Jacques. *The Humiliation of the Word*. Grand Rapids: Eerdmans, 1985.

Evangelical Lutheran Church Cape Town. "Benediction of Disturbance." Facebook, Apr. 23, 2017. https://www.facebook.com/elccapetown/posts/290081098081960/.

Friedman, Steven. *The Reflecting Team in Action*. New York: Guilford, 1995.

Gaum, Laurie, and Chris Jones. *Twelve Members' Court Battle with the Dutch Reformed Church Regarding Same-Sex Relationships: Assuring an Affirmation of Sexual Diversity*. Stellenbosch: African Sun Media, 2021.

Goddard, Allen J. "Hans Ferdinand Bürki in Retrospect: Theology as Spirituality Through the Lens of Memory." *JTSA* 151 (2015) 24–40.

———. "Invitations to Prophetic Integrity in the Evangelical Spirituality of the Students' Christian Association's Discipleship Tradition: 1965–1979." PhD diss., University of KwaZulu-Natal, 2016.

Graeber, David. *Bullshit Jobs: A Theory*. New York: Simon & Schuster, 2018.

Gray, John. *Black Mass: Apocalyptic Religion and the Death of Utopia*. London: Penguin, 2007.

Haffagee, Ferial. "Joburg Is Too Big to Fail. It's Time to Give It Back to Its People." *Daily Maverick*, Aug. 11, 2024. https://www.dailymaverick.co.za/article/2024-08-11-joburg-is-too-big-to-fail-its-time-to-give-it-back-to-its-people/.

Heath, Travis, et al. *Reimagining Narrative Therapy Through Practice Stories and Autoethnography*. London: Routledge, 2022.

Hillman, James. *On Paranoia*. Ascona: Eranos Foundation, 1988.

Holsten, James, and Jaber Gubrium, eds. *Handbook of Constructionist Research*. New York: Guilford, 2007.

Houston, Bill. "Student's Christian Association 1977–1986: Ten Momentous Years and the Movement Towards Integral Mission." *Journal of Theology for Southern Africa* 179 (2024) 33–55.

Jennings, Willie James. *After Whiteness: An Education in Belonging*. Grand Rapids: Eerdmans, 2020.

Kairos South Africa. "The South Africa Kairos Document 1985." WordPress. https://kairossouthernafrica.wordpress.com/2011/05/08/the-south-africa-kairos-document-1985/.

Klein, Naomi. *The Shock Doctrine: The Rise of Disaster Capitalism*. Toronto: Knopf Canada, 2007.

Lederach, John Paul. *The Journey Toward Reconciliation*. Harrisonburg, VA: Herald, 1991.

Louw, A. F. *My Eerste Neëntig Jaar*. Pretoria: N. G. Church Publishers, 1958.

Louw, Daniel J. "On Facing the God-Question in a Pastoral Theology of Compassion: From Imperialistic Omni-Categories to Theopaschitic Pathos-Categories." *In die Skriflig* 49.1 (2015) 1–15.

Mackail, John William, trans. *The Odyssey of Homer.* Cambridge: Cambridge University Press, 2009.

Maimela, Simon S. "An Anthropological Heresy: A Critique of White Theology." In *Apartheid Is a Heresy*, edited by John W. De Gruchy and Charles Villa-Vicencio, 48–58. London: David Philip, 1982.

Meiring, P. G. J. "Reforum: A Brief but Not Unimportant Chapter in the Dutch Reformed Church's Apartheid Saga." *Verbum et Ecclesia* 42.1 (2021) 1–8.

Migliore, Daniel L., ed. *Reading the Gospels with Karl Barth.* Grand Rapids: Eerdmans, 2017.

Modise, Leepo. "The Rocky Road Travelled by the Dutch Reformed Church in Africa Towards Church Unity: From Tshilidzini to Pretoria 1971 to 1991." *Nederduitse Gereformeerde Teologiese Tydskrif* 54.3/4 (September and December 2013) 1–9.

Morgan, Alice. *What Is Narrative Therapy? An Easy-to-Read Introduction.* Adelaide, S. Aus.: Dulwich Centre, 2000.

Motjuwadi, Stan. "The Church Must Speak Up When There Is Injustice." *DRUM* magazine, March 1982, 28–29.

Muofhe, Lillian T., et al. *And We Forgave Them: Stories from the Struggle Against Apartheid in Venda, South Africa.* Hidden Histories Series. Edited by Michael O'Loughlin. Pretoria: Unisa, 2018.

Nolan, Albert. *Jesus Today: A Spirituality of Radical Freedom.* Cape Town: Double Storey, 2006.

Nouwen, Henri J. M., et al. *Compassion: A Reflection on the Christian Life.* New York: Doubleday, 1999.

The Offspring. "The Kids Aren't Alright." *Americana.* Columbia Records, 1998.

O'Hanlon, B. "The Third Wave: Can a Brief Therapy Open Doors to Transformation?" *Family Therapy Networker,* Nov./Dec. 1994, 19–29.

Parliament of the Republic of South Africa. "Parliament Mourns the Passing of Dr Dean Tshenuwani Simon Farisani, Former Member of Parliament." May 29, 2025. https://www.parliament.gov.za/index.php/press-releases/media-release-parliament-mourns-passing-dr-dean-tshenuwani-simon-farisani-former-member-parliament.

Paton, Alan. *Cry, the Beloved Country.* New York: Simon & Schuster, 2003.

Perkinson, James. "Like a Thief in the Night: Black Theology and White Church in the Third Millennium." *Theology Today* 60.4 (2004) 508–24.

———. *White Theology: Outing Supremacy in Modernity.* London: Palgrave Macmillan, 2004.

Philpott, Margaret. "The Death of Tshifhiwa Muofhe." *South African History Online*, 2017. https://www.sahistory.org.za/archive/death-tshifhiwa-muofhe-margaret-philpott.

Rambo, Shelly. *Spirit and Trauma: A Theology of Remaining.* Louisville, KY: Westminster John Knox, 2010.

Rohr, Richard. *Everything Belongs: The Gift of Contemplative Prayer.* New York: Crossroad, 1999.

Roszak, Theodore. *The Voice of the Earth.* New York: Simon & Schuster, 1992.

———. *Where the Wasteland Ends: Politics and Transcendence in Post Industrial Society.* Garden City, NY: Doubleday, 1973.

Shakespeare, William. "All the World's a Stage." Poetry Foundation. https://www.poetryfoundation.org/poems/56966/speech-all-the-worlds-a-stage.

Singata, Silakhe. "Justice for the Dead." *Stellenbosch Theological Journal* 6.4 (2020) 319–45. https://doi.org/10.17570/stj.2020.v6n4.a13.

Smith, Nico. *Tshilidzini: Christian Missionary Work in an Apartheid Context.* Privately published by Maretha Laubscher, 2017.

Southern Cross. "White SA Church Leaders Respond to Trump." *Southern Cross*, Feb. 13, 2025. https://www.scross.co.za/2025/02/white-sa-church-leaders-respond-to-trump/.

Thurman, Howard. *The Luminous Darkness: A Personal Interpretation of the Anatomy of Segregation and the Ground of Hope.* Richmond, Indiana: Friends United, 1989.

Tutu, Desmond. *No Future Without Forgiveness.* New York: Random House, 1999.

Van Aarde, Andries. *Fatherless in Galilee.* London: Continuum, 2001.

Van Wyngaard, G. J. (Cobus). *In Search of Repair: Critical Responses to Whiteness as a Theological Problem—A South African Contribution.* PhD diss., Vrije Universiteit Amsterdam, 2019.

Van Wyngaard, G. J. (Cobus), and Marius Louw. "Theology from the Suburbs: The Challenge of Life for the City as a Whole." *International Journal of Public Theology* 17 (2023) 477–96.

Van Zyl, Mikki, and Melissa Steyn, eds. *Performing Queer: Shaping Sexualities 1994–2004.* Social Identities South Africa Series 1. Roggebaai, South Africa: Kwela, 2005.

Vivanco, Esti. "Johannes Vermeer's Influence and Inspiration." WordPress, May 15, 2011. https://vermeer0708.wordpress.com/2011/05/15/johannes-vermeers-woman-holding-a-balance-a-general-review/.

www.ingramcontent.com/pod-product-compliance
Lightning Source LLC
LaVergne TN
LVHW020636100826
845148LV00012B/2199

* 9 7 9 8 3 8 5 2 5 7 1 7 1 *